The Underlying Order

KATHLEEN RAINE

The Underlying Order
and other essays

EDITED WITH AN INTRODUCTION
BY BRIAN KEEBLE

TEMENOS ACADEMY

TEMENOS ACADEMY PAPERS NO. 30

First published 2008 by
The Temenos Academy
16 Lincoln's Inn Fields
London WC2A 3ED

www.temenosacademy.org

Registered Charity no. 1043015

ISBN 978 0 9551934 6 0

Typeset by
Agnesi Text, Hadleigh
Printed in the United Kingdom at
Smith Settle, Yeadon

The Temenos Academy
wishes to express its deep gratitude
to The Ven. John Weaver, OBE,
(8 March 1911 – 5 July 2008),
for generously sponsoring the
publication of this book.

This gift to Temenos is made in memory
of The Right Reverend Herman Page,
Bishop of the Diocese of Michigan,
and of The Right Reverend Herman R. Page,
Bishop of the Diocese of Northern Michigan.

¶ Contents

ℐ Introduction

This small gathering of six previously uncollected essays is intended by the Temenos Academy to mark the centenary of the birth of its Founder, the poet Kathleen Raine – born 14 June 1908. During a long life—she died 6 July 2003—Kathleen was a prolific poet, essayist, scholar, reviewer and sometime editor and translator and, increasingly with maturity, a champion of standards and values she equated with the Perennial Philosophy. Having let it be known that she regarded modernism as having severe inadequacies, mainly due to its being based upon the purely materialist and quantitative premisses of modern science, the poet was by degrees marginalized by the literary establishment. This had the effect of deepening and adding to the fervour with which she gave expression to those meanings and values she held to be requisite for a legitimate culture. These meanings and values she saw as being embedded in what she called—to use her own portmanteau phrase—the 'Learning of the Imagination'. Integral to this learning was a knowledge of how almost all past cultures, and certainly all those worthy of the name, have acknowledged the necessity for the various arts to embody in their practice a vision of life that includes, as both the root and flowering of the natural order, noumenal orders of reality. A vision of reality that does not include a knowledge of the spiritual was for this author not only a truncation, but on that account a perversion and a betrayal.

In this, of course, Kathleen Raine was far from the presumptions and assumptions of modernism, based as her view was on a doctrine of man as being created, however it might be coloured by religious and cultural circumstances, in the Divine Image. As a poet herself and in this light, it must have been pre-ordained that she would become a profound scholar of Blake's works as well as of his 'student' Yeats. It also explains her championing those of her contemporaries whose imaginative experience resonated beyond an exclusively human, sensory perception of the world: Edwin Muir, Vernon Watkins, David Jones and Cecil Collins among others.

Being, as she was, increasingly at odds with whatever was fashionably acceptable in cultural circles, and although she certainly addressed audiences at the highest intellectual level— at Eranos, for instance and in France and India where she was especially valued—gradually she gathered around her and addressed audiences that were of a like persuasion: that is to say, were not academic (indeed, they were frequently the disaffected from their ranks), but were nonetheless serious, often learned and matched her ardent defence of the perennial values and meanings that are the heart of the legacy of past cultures—those superior to our own.

Sharing her aspirations in this direction naturally lead to the founding, with Philip Sherrard, Keith Critchlow and myself, of the journal *Temenos* in 1980. Later, in her eighties, Kathleen undertook the immense labour of founding in 1991 the Temenos Academy: and some years later still the *Temenos Academy Review*. It was to audiences likely to attend the Academy's lectures and seminars (and give them) and, perhaps further afield, read the *Review*, and to audiences of a similar cultural and intellectual ambience that all but one of the papers collected here were delivered. These were papers addressed primarily to an audience for whom their author believed what mattered about the arts is that they are above all a *lived* experience: not something we learn *about* but the very source *from* which we might learn what the transformative energies of imaginative vision might contribute to the integral wholeness of life itself. For instance, note with what impassioned reverence the author argues the more than literary or psychological values of those affinities with the world of nature on which Wordsworth built his most revered poetry.

All this I have considered when editing these papers. I have kept in mind that they were (with the exception of the Donne) meant to be heard rather than studied. For this reason I have not cluttered them with footnotes and references, except for a bare minimum beyond what the author has supplied—and those mostly to the Donne essay. My chief concern has been to establish an accurate text, particularly for the quotations, since the author was here over-relying on her prodigious yet faulty memory. As is often the case in such circumstances, I have found it necessary to make an occasional cut in order to avoid repetition.

I have included the 'early' Donne essay partly because of its intrinsic merit and partly because it is about a poet one does not readily associate with Kathleen Raine. Handing me a copy of it a few years before she died—'for your archives'—she dismissed it as 'too clever by half in an Eliotish sort of way'. That reservation notwithstanding, it seems to me that it should have an airing here, for a readership far removed from its original. Moreover, the essay does incidentally serve as a marker of the distance travelled from the 'early' paper to the late papers that make up the bulk of this collection.

I had thought to include a second paper on Shelley. Kathleen was early on a champion of his work, as well we might expect, at a time when he was deeply unfashionable and one spoke with enthusiasm about him at some risk to one's own poetic reputation. Since then this most rhapsodic of the Romantics has been somewhat rehabilitated. The rejected paper, 'Shelley and the India of the Imagination', can be found in *Indian Horizons* (vol. 41, no. 4, Delhi, 1992, pp. 17–35). There is still some interest and pleasure to be had by comparing the two. They reveal how the author, working more or less from a single core reading of selected passages, demonstrates in one the indebtedness to Indian doctrine of the metaphysics of Shelley's shaping of certain characters contained in, for instance, *Prometheus Unbound, Hellas* and *Epipsychidion*, and in the other the influence of Indian doctrine in animating the imaginative impetus of Shelley's mythologizing powers. The latter is clearly a reworking of the former using some of the same passages of quotation. However, in the end the overlap between the two papers proved intractable, deciding me in favour of including the paper here since it has not, so far as I know, been published hitherto.

*

'Nature and Meaning' was first delivered as a paper at a Resurgence Weekend at Edinburgh, June 1986. It was revised and published as 'Common Ground', in *Resurgence*, no. 119 (November–December 1982), pp. 8–12. This revision is reproduced here.

'The Underlying Order' was originally written for the 1985 Conference of the Centre for Spiritual Studies. It was subsequently published in *Fragments of Infinity: Essays in Religion and Philosophy*, a *Festschrift* in honour of Professor Huston Smith, edited by Arvind Sharma, Prism Press (1991), pp. 198–216.

'A Sense of Beauty' was first given as a paper at a symposium held by the Kairos Foundation, London, whose aim is 'to investigate study, record and promote traditional values of science and art'. The text published here appeared in *Resurgence*, no. 114 (January–February 1986), pp. 8–12.

'John Donne and the Baroque Doubt' is reprinted from *Horizon*, vol. xi, no. 66 (June 1945), pp. 371–95.

'Shelley as a Mythological Poet' was read as a paper to the Temenos Academy, 1997. It is previously unpublished except for a limited edition of ten copies in an A4 ring-binder format with four colour illustrations of Indian miniatures, 'printed at the Anchorhold (Haywards Heath) for the Temenos Academy, 1997'.

'Wordsworth—a Remembered Experience' is reproduced here from an undated photocopy of an original typescript in the editor's possession and is possibly the text of a talk given to the Wordsworth Trust in 2000.

On this, as on previous occasions, I am indebted to Jack Herbert and Grevel Lindop for their help. The Temenos Academy is grateful to Faber and Faber Limited for permission to quote David Jones's 'A, a, Domine Deus'.

Brian Keeble, August 2008

§ I

⟨ Nature and Meaning

At the time I reached the sixth form at school I had to make the choice that comes to all sixth-formers—that momentous parting of the ways—between 'arts' and 'science'. My secret purpose was to be a poet, but I nevertheless chose to read botany and zoology because nature was my theme and I wanted to know everything about it. I felt, besides, that poetry and literature in general were not 'subjects' to be studied and learned but the stuff of life: the literature of our own language we can all read for ourselves. I also felt that about my fellow poets I needed no one's judgement or instruction but my own. Years later C. S. Lewis asked me—I was back at Girton at the time as a Research Fellow and he had arrived as Regius Professor of English—if I had ever learned anything from any work of literary criticism. I answered that I never had, and he said neither had he. Scholarship, which provides facts relevant to the study of some work of literature or some period in the history of ideas, is another matter. In any case I would not have accepted intervention in an area of my life which must remain inviolate.

Whatever my reasons I made the right choice: I have learned more about poetry from my mother, from my friends, from solitude, and from the school of life than I could ever have done from the Cambridge English School, which has done so much harm to the reading of poetry in my generation and after. The leaden cloud of 'scientific criticism' obscured my own vision for years to come as it was. But what I learned of the structures and patternings of 'nature' has remained for me an insight of wonder. However, I did not

follow the straight road on which my education might have
set me—nor did I ever at heart intend to do so—but pursued
my own crooked road which made itself. Today I would like to
return to that parting of the ways and consider 'nature' as the
common ground of poet and scientist, and indeed of all of us;
it is our shared world, into which we are born, of which we
are, even if we live in the most congested inner city area, a
part, and which is a part of us. There are many ways of seeing
and understanding nature, but it seems that at this time science
has laid claim to a monopoly in the understanding of nature to
which it has no just claim; and poetry has itself become in-
fected by the outlook of a materialist science to the point of
losing its own vision and forgetting its own task. This seems to
me a question worth studying at a conference of *Resurgence*
readers, for *Resurgence* is concerned with all that is green, and
the use we make of our green earth, not in material terms
alone but also as the house in which we live imaginatively,
which gives the soul as well as the body all that it needs.

Much bad modern verse is uncritically and unquestioningly
based in materialist premisses because those who write it
have simply adopted current attitudes and assumptions without even being aware of any alternative; I remember T. S. Eliot
saying that the most dangerous influences are unconscious
influences; and I might add that these are also the strongest.
Certain assumptions are in our world so little questioned as
to seem unquestionable. I am speaking of premisses, which
have more and more come to be established on the foundations of a materialist science. In the Communist world dialec-
tical materialism has come, as we know, to occupy the place of
a religion. As such there has been a good deal of reaction
against it, sometimes heroic. But the unquestioned assumptions of materialism are no less widespread in the capitalist
West, whose machines are the idols of the capitalist system

also, to which our society is enslaved and whose power to destroy us grows daily greater by what seems an autonomous and irreversible process. But in reality if we ourselves withdraw our worship from those idols they will be powerless. We don't have to live in a world of machines manufacturing machines, of which weapons and destruction are the most profitable and the most powerful—this is a choice our civilization has made. Other civilizations, grounded in different premises, have made different choices; and a future civilization, if we survive this one, must and will choose other means to different ends. I am concerned, therefore, not with breaking the machines but with questioning the ideology which has given rise to them.

I don't propose to go into history and how we have come to be where we are, confronting the situation which we must resolve. Perhaps with Aristotle, perhaps with the Renaissance, with the Royal Society, with Bacon and Newton, with Descartes, the West has shown a bias towards the study of nature— the object of knowledge—at the expense of mind, the knower. So that for most Western people the outer world presents, even now that science has itself recognized that this is far from being so, the aspect of a solid, substantial reality, made of something called 'matter'—not so solid nowadays—which is entirely separate from our observing minds although our bodies are themselves parts of the great cosmic mechanism, governed by 'laws of nature'. Given this divorce between inner and outer worlds the idea of a God has, very naturally, lost all meaning because the notion that some being must have 'made' the mechanism as a watch-maker might make a watch, then set it going of its own accord, has come to seem superfluous. Nature, so it is now supposed, operates by 'laws' which our sciences have discovered and traced, as it seems, to the very frontiers of the measurable and the quantifiable. The phenomena which we perceive—which we see and hear and touch—have by a process of quantification been reduced to facts, objects, things, having in themselves neither meaning nor value. Indeed to attribute to these facts of nature either meanings or values is, in terms of our materialist science, either childish make-believe or a sin against the scientific virtue of totally detached objectivity. Man has made himself into a machine for measuring and manipulating facts in this era which René Guénon has described in the title of a book in which he challenges it, 'The Reign of Quantity'. And so it has remained until within recent years it has become clear to the scientists working at the frontiers of the measurable that the mind of the observer is a factor which cannot, however objective we may seek to be, be excluded. What might have been clear from the outset has been clear from the outset in, for example, traditional Indian philosophy.

But premisses are not immutable. Once we have identified them we may examine them, and once we have examined them we can see their limitations and their limits. We may even discard them. We can see nature with equal justice not as an object, a thing, but as an experience of the knower. Even scientific knowledge is so, but of nature as an experience there is much more to be known than the scientific method can tell us, and that includes, above all, the realm of poetry and the other arts. I would not wish to deny the value of the immense body of knowledge science has gathered, giving us power over nature, heaven knows, far beyond our wisdom to use that power. Power, as we know, corrupts, and absolute power corrupts absolutely; and this, we can all see, applies to our collective power to manipulate nature.

In challenging Western materialism I am not saying simply that we should not want so many useless possessions and

ought to give more to the Third World or any other of the
excellent causes which abound. All that may be true but, after
all, in a world that lives by manufacturing and selling goods,
creating markets for all kinds of trash by making people want
things they do not need and which can in no way enrich their
lives, holy poverty whether that of Jesus or of the Buddha is
not likely to be popular with our masters in a consumerist
society. But let that pass—the human reasons, the poet's
reasons for calling in question the materialist ideology are of
quite another kind: in making of the world an impersonal
mechanism, devoid of life, we destroy all possibility of a living
relationship with nature, of discovering in its ever-changing
panorama of appearances either meaning or value or beauty,
or anything of what used to be called the Holy. For in a universe of merely material fact all these are irrelevant and
superfluous; are make-believe. Nothing is sacred, nothing has
meaning, nothing has value: only utility. We can manipulate
nature but it has ceased to be something we can love, in whose
aspect we can find meanings, messages that speak to us from
bird and cloud and field and mountain. Nature is no longer a
language that speaks to us, because there is no speaker. That
greatest of naturalists, Charles Darwin, who as a young man
delighted in poetry and music, in his old age sadly wrote that
these had ceased to move him at all. A lifetime of collecting
facts, of deliberately eliminating from his responses to the
natural world all value judgements, all emotions, all feelings,
all the immemorial human sense that everything in the world
from the stars to the birds, from the small mantis of the
African Bushmen to the hills to whose high solitudes the
psalmist looked for help—had for him emptied that world of
all meaning save that of fact, of the measurable, the quantifiable. And such is the picture of 'reality' presented by our
Western, materialist science. Science is 'real' knowledge, while

poetry is something for children, or for psychotherapy, a primitive way of looking at nature which we 'evolved' beings have outgrown. Coleridge wrote of 'that willing suspension of disbelief that constitutes poetic faith'. But why is 'disbelief' such a mental virtue that only by suspending it can we indulge in an evening of poetic make-believe? But if poetry is make-believe it is in any case worthless.

Yet in these responses that science would have us eliminate from the field of what we call knowledge do we not find the very essence of our human nature? Is not the realm of meanings and of values, of the old verities of truth, beauty and goodness, the measure of our humanity? We do not only quantify, we evaluate, and values are immeasurable. A mechanism has no value or meaning; it has only utility. It performs its function. By making of 'nature' a machine we banish it from life and can no longer love it. Blake, who above all others has challenged the premises of materialism, well understood this when he wrote: 'Think of a white cloud as being holy, you cannot love it; but think of a holy man within the cloud, love springs up in your thoughts, for to think of holiness distinct from man is impossible to the affections. Thought alone can make monsters, but the affections cannot.'

Blake himself believed that 'Cloud, meteor and star / Are men seen afar', that all nature is informed by the divine humanity he calls 'Jesus, the Imagination'. All things exist in the living imagination which experiences them, and are thus 'human, mighty, sublime'. This is not the time or place to set forth the philosophic principles which underlie this alternative view to that of mechanistic science. Suffice it to say that such is the philosophy of the Vedas and the Upanishads, of Plato and the Neoplatonists, indeed of all philosophic systems other than that of the modern West during the last three and a half centuries—a 'provincial' deviation, as Yeats understood it, from unanimous and universal tradition. At last we are beginning to understand the mechanical theory for what it is, a limited and limiting hypothesis, already obsolete. Yeats believed that a change was already beginning—'The three provincial centuries are over,' he wrote to a friend; 'wisdom and poetry return.' He was Blake's first editor, and Blake was his master. Blake's point is simple enough—we cannot love a thing, an object, a mechanism, we can love only a living being, a Person. If nature is made into a mechanism we are doomed to live in a world we cannot love, a world which communicates no meaning, no values. Beauty becomes a sentimental and meaningless word, whereas for Plato it expressed the deepest truth of his philosophic understanding.

But have we not even now reached the end of the mechanistic theory which makes a separation between knower and known, seer and seen, the human mind and spirit and external nature, that epiphany of marvels ever-changing and moving before our eyes? The old search for the secret of the *unus mundus* has returned in a new form; no longer need we see man as an insignificant spare part in a mindless mechanism, but rather the cosmos and the human akin because informed with the one life, in which the inner universe finds perpetually its correspondence in the outer world, a natural world which is an expression of the one mind that moves through all things, from stone and star to plants, animals, flowers, which are all, as we are ourselves, living expressions of that living mind. Do we not return full circle to that neglected and despised primitive experience Laurens van der Post found in the African Bushmen, of a universe living in all its parts and in its whole; 'There is a dream dreaming us,' as a bushman said to him. As against the universe as a mechanism do we not return to the universe as a being, and the world, in Plato's words, 'an immortal and happy living being', a Person not a machine?

Poetry, then, becomes not a primitive and inexact mode of factual knowledge superseded by natural science, heaven help us, but a true knowledge, at once sight and insight, at once hearing and understanding of the continual epiphany of forms opening every moment before us the mystery of being in which we participate. A mystery not in the current sense of a problem to be solved in the manner of Sherlock Holmes, but in the older sense of a reality which in its depths lies beyond human understanding. 'Man can embody truth but he cannot know it,' Yeats wrote. That in which we live and move and have our being is not something that science has not as yet 'solved'. Life cannot be explained by the discovery of the genetic code, that much publicized little triumph of human ingenuity, but is something not in its nature soluble by the quantitative method.

Nature then becomes a language that we can read, and the poet one skilled in the reading of the natural world which mirrors continually the meanings of our own nature, of our feelings and thoughts. Nature gives us a language both complex and subtle, grand and terrible, beautiful and holy, ageless and ever new, in which we may discern deep truths which are our own truths of heart and spirit. There is no human mood of delight or melancholy, of fear or joy, which we may not discover in that mirror; man the microcosm can know the universe only in our own image for outer and inner worlds are one. Thus the true poetry of nature is not what passes as 'nature poetry' in a secular world—descriptions more or less detailed of the appearances of things—but a poetry in which nature is itself the language to which we listen and through which we receive those communications in which, in Blake's

words, 'the Cloud the River & the Field Talk with the husbandman & shepherd'. Blake well understood that the mind of
the reasoner—that blind, unhappy mentality characterized as
Urizen, the mind of the empirical ego—loses this faculty and
that instead of the phenomena of nature instructing him,
'these attacked him sore', for nature becomes alien and inim-
ical and remote to the mechanistic scientist as Darwin found
to his cost and his sorrow, without, however, discerning that
the source of this alienation lies in that very 'scientific method'
on whose purity he prided himself.

I have criticized a certain widespread and popular kind of
modern poetry as being itself coloured by the materialist
ideology whose premisses are unquestioned in our current
secular culture. Such writers depict a material universe devoid
of meanings and values, a rather distasteful commonplace to
which (such poetry implies) it is courageous and honest to
come to terms because that is 'reality'. You may describe in
detail some physical event or the physical appearance of a dead
fish or an inner city area, but coldly and without love, without
the sense of the numinous or the holy, without the sense of a
larger whole or of inner dimensions of which even the dead
fish or the inner city area is part. Photographic precision of
detail is the measure of the poet's skill, and a kind of knowing
cynicism which reduces all to the commonplace of his 'honesty' and, it is implied, his or her social commitment. It stresses
the immediate surroundings of the kitchen sink, the dead fish,
or the fish queue, as the real 'world' that people inhabit. Such
is the 'truth' of secular materialism; whereas Milton's or
Shelley's or Keats's or Hopkins's or Vernon Watkins's or any
other poet of the imagination's deeper insight is dismissed as
untruth, as make-believe. So the soul is starved and condemned to live in the mean habitation of a reductionist, and
finally a nihilist zero of the heart and spirit.

Such verse—I cannot call it poetry—corresponds to the premisses of the current materialist culture and its assumptions and expectations but does nothing to nourish the heart or the soul, or in Blake's words 'to open the eternal worlds' which are our true universe. Such work fulfils no function at all which cannot be done as well or better in a news bulletin or a social survey or weather report. Critics have always liked to condemn Plato for banishing from his Republic naturalistic poets, but I suggest that he did so not because he did not think poetry had a function but because he considered that such poets were not fulfilling that function; and the same is true today and for the same reasons. 'One thing alone makes a poet,' Blake wrote, 'Imagination, the Divine Vision.' To obscure or deny that vision in verse is not to be a poet. The calling of the poet is indeed a sacred one, but only in so far as the poet performs that sacred task of speaking to the human imagination in its own language, of the eternal order and harmony of which all being is a manifestation. For those who like their news and social surveys in verse, well and good, but I suggest that this is not poetry and has no bearing on the true function of the arts which is to nourish the human spirit, to build the invisible house of the soul. Vernon Watkins on a visit to Yeats in the spring of 1938, not long before the poet's death, quoted Auden as saying, 'A poem must contain news and a poet must be something of a reporter', to which Yeats replied, 'The reverse is true', and then added, 'That attitude to poetry is just materialism.' If poetry were as the secular view would have us believe, it would be entirely useless, superfluous.

The prevalence in our society of a poetry of 'celebration of the commonplace' (the phrase is David Gascoyne's) might seem to be an expression of 'the century of the common man' and to show a proper respect and appreciation of the 'common man' of the age. But is this really so? I suggest that the common man—and woman and, above all, child—is gravely misconceived and undervalued by those materialist ideologies which purvey the vulgar, the trivial, the reductionist caricature of the human image that arises not at all from the noble democratic ideal to which the media claim to subscribe, but to the denial of the common man's eternal nature and spiritual dignity inherent in all materialist ideologies whether Marxist or those of the Western consumerist society. Why should the 'kitchen sink' be deemed more real, more inherently democratic and egalitarian than the sun and the stars, trees and birds and flowers, seas and mountains, day and night, birth and love and death, which are common to all? Is it not from the loss of the vision of man's real nature that what is most universal is excluded? Man is not common. But the ideologies which dominate our consumerist societies play on only the lowest values in order to sell their commodities, the trash of the machines. Total humanity is not the prerogative of any social group; rather it is our ideologies which distort, falsify and reduce the image and the experience of human dignity. Too many contemporary poets and other artists fail in their task of showing images, not of the commonplace but of the universal—the human image in its true lineaments of 'mercy, pity, peace and love' and 'nature' as a perpetual epiphany of the spirit of life. 'If the salt has lost its savour, wherewith shall it be salted?'

Or again, consider the discrepancy which the materialist standpoint introduces between the variety and scope of feelings and responses of which the human soul is capable—the range and scale of perceptions, intuitions, moods of delight or terror, awe, the sense of the holy, of the numinous—and the universe which materialist ideologies present as nothing but a mechanism operating by blind collisions of material particles or forces. For what purpose then—and in what manner—have we come to possess these rich and varied powers, this scale of responses, of modes of experiencing and understanding our universe and one another? It is as if we were to say of a bird in its shell that wings, eyes, all the organs of its life to be, corresponded to nothing in its world. Nor do they, until the bird takes flight in its own proper skies. So our marvellous capacity for experience must relate to a universe in which the full gamut of these responses is appropriate and valid. To deny the life, the meanings, the values, in the last instance the holiness of nature is to deny ourselves wings and eyes to experience that world so rich in qualities which respond to those meanings and values which we are imaginatively equipped to comprehend and express. It is to make the albatross walk on the ground and to make the swallow live in the house of the mole. These age-old practices of meditation and prayer by which humankind has traditionally found attunement to what is beyond and about and within us, no longer have any meaning: for to whom or to what can we 'lift up our hearts'? If a creature possesses an organ there must be in nature that situation to which the organ corresponds. And so with human consciousness, our universe cannot lack these correspondences of powers innate in us. These cannot be quantified, in their very nature; but to deny what cannot be quantified is to degrade, to mutilate, to coarsen our quality of being. 'Conduct and work grow coarse, and coarse the soul,' Yeats wrote—inevitably so, as he well understood, if we seek to live by the mechanistic theory. We have but to go to almost any exhibition of modern art, to pick up any school anthology of modern verse, to see the coarseness of work and soul that derives from a materialist view of man. As the painter Francis Bacon has said, it is now known to all that 'man is an accident' and that all art is just a game. One hears this said on radio programmes as a generally received truth. But Yeats saw further, saw the beginning of the swing of the gyres of history away from our naïve materialism: having reached the extremest distance from the spiritual source, where 'the falcon cannot hear the falconer', we begin to experience the change, the swing back. That, it seems to me, is where we are now. While for the majority, the media persons and their faithful followers, the mechanism goes on, there are everywhere to be found little, secret cells of a new life beginning to take its new form. And as we know *Resurgence*—the very name speaks of a renewal of life—is one of these.

I have recently been re-reading—and not for the first or the second time—the poems of Vernon Watkins, whose Collected Poems have belatedly appeared nearly twenty years after his death. To read his poetry alive with seas and birds, foal in spring sunlight, sycamore with its roots in the graves, the rhythms and mysteries of the living and the dead, is to be caught up in the very rhythms and music of creation itself. And if many find his poetry 'difficult' I suggest that this is because we have allowed our responsiveness to fall into disuse and not because our world's tides and seasons, growth and decay spell meanings beyond the comprehension of the common man. Those who want the commonplace, Vernon held (as his conversation with Yeats indicates), have no need to ask the poets to supply it. The journalists can do that for us. It is for the poet, Vernon held, to open the eyes of vision, to show us the universe that gave us birth and opens for us the mystery also of death, of whose life we are a part not as cogs in a machine but as single lives within the divine life that informs all. As against Francis Bacon's view that man is an accident and all art just a game, I would remind you of the Indian vision of the divine spirit—the God—at play in all life, a breath breathing through all things. Yeats and Blake were Vernon Watkins's masters, a copy of MacKenna's Plotinus lay on his desk when I visited him at his house at Pennard, on the Gower Peninsula, so close to the sea and air and stars that it seemed caught up in the elemental universe. He was, as we know, a deep and life-long Christian. Need we cling to the kitchen sink as if that were more real and nearer to us than the music of the spheres and the eternal nature of the human spirit, present in all?

It's really a question of love. You cannot love human beings, in the long run, if these are seen as mere mechanisms of con-ditioned reflexes—as the Behaviourist psychology, still so popular in America and elsewhere, depicts them. To make of human beings objects, mechanisms, is the last betrayal of our human nature, but it is also the logical term of the secular materialism we accept so unquestioningly. Materialist art is a loveless art, materialist poetry a loveless poetry. A materialist world is a loveless world. I suggested in a recent issue of *Resurgence* [see 'A Sense of Beauty' herein] that beauty is the aspect of things loved. But that is no facile sentimentality, for I now suggest that we cannot love what does not possess life, that we must rediscover that we participate in a living universe, or perish by and with our machines. 'Everything that lives is holy,' Blake says; nothing that does not possess that holy life is sacred, we can see on every side in the characteristic produc-tions of the machine age, in the violence and coarseness of the life it inspires, the sad poverty of human relationships, in marriage, in relations between the generations, and of course between societies and groups within our societies. *Resurgence* stands for the living earth and its right uses, and that is not something that can be restricted to utilitarian considerations— that our natural resources are running out, that the feeding of our human population is a problem that must be solved, in terms of productivity, control of pollution and so on. For these considerations must, as E. F. Schumacher so well understood, go hand in hand with a change of values, with a rediscovery of the earth as sacred, as the God-given house not of our bodies only but of our souls.

☙ The Underlying Order: Nature and the Imagination

It is heartening to see that at last the long unquestioned assumptions of naïve materialism that have dominated the modern Western world are beginning to seem less certain, less self-evident than they were even a few years ago. When I was a student—more than fifty years ago—I was torn between two possible choices. I intended to be a poet—that was certain—and it seemed therefore obvious to those who advised me that I should read English Literature at university. But to me this was by no means obvious. I felt I had no need to seek the opinions of others on my fellow writers, and I have had no reason to regret my decision to read instead natural sciences. For that was the other alternative. Always, from infancy—and in this I was perhaps no different from every child born into this marvellous world—nature had been my passion, and I thought I could best learn to contemplate and know its inexhaustible order and meaning by becoming a botanist or a marine biologist. But my love of nature was really a poet's love for meaning and beauty, rather than for fact or for manipulations and applications of scientific knowledge for practical ends. I found great delight in my studies of nature at that time, in contemplating that order and beauty that is to be found throughout the whole structure of the world, whether as it appears to the eye, or in those minute worlds revealed by microscope or beyond the visible altogether. But my love of these things was a poet's love first and last. When a year or two ago one of my granddaughters showed me one of her examination papers in botany and asked me which questions

I could answer, I had to say that once I could have answered question 4 but none of the others! For science, knowledge is ever changing; what is 'knowledge' when we are young is no longer when we are old.

But poetry and the other arts relate to the everlasting. One might say that all art is contemporaneous, the cave paintings of Lascaux with those of Ajanta and Ellora; Greek classical sculpture with that of Chartres; the music of Monteverdi is not superseded by that of Mozart or of Wagner; Murasaki is as close to us as Marcel, the people of Shakespeare, with Homer's Hector and Achilles, with Rama and Arjuna, and all these are ourselves.

Orthodoxy, in our world, means scientific orthodoxy, and although the conclusions of science in some particular area may be open to question, the premisses of the materialist ideology are not. To question these is to invite exclusion from any discussion whatsoever. As I understand it, science as we know it presumes a universe which consists of something called 'matter', which, whatever else may be said about it, is measurable, quantifiable, and constitutes an ordered and autonomous system, coherent and unified in all its parts and as a whole, the space–time continuum of the universe. Newton— and psychologically do we not still live in the Newtonian era?—conceived the material universe to be a mechanism functioning autonomously by the so-called 'laws of nature' which are the Ten Commandments, so to speak, of science. Within this great self-coherent order, value judgements are superfluous. It is 'unscientific' to attribute to 'nature' any purposes, or qualities; any of those invisible and immeasurable human qualities such as joy and sorrow and love, or meaning of whatever kind. The human mind, according to Locke (the philosopher of the Newtonian system) thus becomes 'passive before a mechanized nature'. These words are Yeats's, who was a disciple of Blake, the sole lonely prophet to call in question, at the end of the eighteenth century, this whole structure of thought.

Thus the materialist hypothesis—for it is no more—attributes order and reality to the outer world, leaving mind itself, consciousness itself, as the mere mirror or receptacle of impressions. All knowledge comes from without, the mind of an infant is a blank page on which these impressions can be written. Human beings are themselves conceived as mechanisms activated by so-called reflexes—mindless parts of a mindless material order, with consciousness itself degraded to a mere attribute of matter. Paradoxically, machines are treated as if these possessed human qualities, computers as if they possessed 'knowledge', even as the brain is treated as a short-lived computer. Such assumptions, consciously or unconsciously held, continue in a large measure to determine the kind and quality of the world we live in. Yet we are in reality living in a world whose assumptions and values rest on the no longer tenable hypothesis that 'nature' operates in independence of the perceiving mind, and is itself the source and the object of all knowledge. The great regions of consciousness itself are deemed unreal because immeasurable. The mind is popularly identified with the brain; knowledge is stored away in right or left lobes as it is in a computer; you can tell that people are meditating or dreaming by affixing electrical apparatus to their heads, but what does that tell us of *what* is thought, or of the dream itself, or of the *experience* of meditation? Nothing at all. The human kingdom—the kingdom of consciousness—is excluded by definitions which see the real as identical with the measurable. It is not our conclusions but our premises that are false. We might even reverse them and say that reality is what we experience, and that all experience is immeasurable.

According to another view—and we must remember that

this is the view the Eastern world, in various forms, has held over millennia—'nature' is a system of appearances whose ground is consciousness itself. Science measures the phenomena which we perceive, and which Indian philosophical systems call *māyā*. *Māyā* has sometimes been termed illusion, but it is, more exactly, appearances. Blake used the word 'visions': this world, he wrote, 'is one continued vision of fancy or imagination'. But if the materialist premisses are reversed, then 'reality' is not material fact but meaning itself. And it follows that in those civilizations grounded on this premiss—our own included up to the Renaissance—the arts, as expressions of the value system of a culture, have been held in high regard as expressions of knowledge of the highest order. Is not our human kingdom in its very nature a universe of meanings and values? For these are inherent in life itself, as such, the Vedantic *sat-chit-ananda,* being-consciousness-bliss: being *is* consciousness, and the third term *ananda* (bliss) is the ultimate value of being and consciousness. We are made for beatitude, as the theologians would say; Freud, indeed, said something not dissimilar when he spoke of the fundamental nature of 'the pleasure principle' as the goal all seek. Plotinus wrote of 'felicity' as the goal and natural term of all life, and attributed it not only to man and animals but to plants also. Beatitude— felicity—is not an accident of being and consciousness: it is our very nature to seek, and to attain, joy; and it is for the arts to hold before us images of our eternal nature, through which we may awaken to, and grow towards, that reality which is our humanity itself.

This view of reality Blake defended in its darkest hour, at the end of the rationalist eighteenth century and the beginning of the materialist nineteenth. Few heeded him or understood him when he said, 'All that I see is vision', and 'To me this world is one continued vision of imagination.' That is the sort of thing unpractical poets and painters do say! But Blake was in earnest and spoke as a metaphysician sure of his ground when he wrote of the living sun:

> 'What', it will be Question'd, 'When the Sun rises, do you not see a round disk of fire somewhat like a Guinea?' O no, no, I see an Innumerable company of the Heavenly host crying 'Holy, Holy, Holy is the Lord God Almighty'. I question not my Corporeal or Vegetative Eye any more than I would Question a Window concerning a Sight. I look thro' it and not with it.

Plato had used the same words about looking 'through not with' the eye. And what else, after all, could that innumerable multitude of beings proclaim, being themselves not objects in a lifeless mechanism, but an epiphany of life which not only has, but is, being, consciousness and bliss? The real, therefore, is ultimately—and this again has been understood by all traditions—not an object but a person. A 'Person' in this sense not by a human act of personification of something in its innate reality neither living nor conscious; but rather human 'persons' are a manifestation in multitude of the single person of Being itself, from which consciousness and meaning are inseparable, these being innate qualities of life itself, as such. Not 'life' as a property of matter, but life as experienced. 'Everything that lives is holy' summarizes Blake's total vision of reality—not holy because we choose to think it so, but intrinsically so. The 'holy' is, again, a reality that cannot be defined but can be experienced as the ultimate knowledge of consciousness. It cannot be measured, but neither can it be denied, if by knowledge we mean what is experienced. Within the scope of human experience there are degrees of knowledge and value, self-authenticating, of which those who have reached the farthest regions tell us, the vision of the holy, and the beatitude of that vision is the highest term. And therefore Blake's stars and grains of sand can say no other than 'Holy, Holy, Holy'.

> To see a World in a Grain of Sand
> And a Heaven in a Wild Flower,
> Hold Infinity in the palm of your hand
> And Eternity in an hour.

That is not poetic fancy: it is profoundest knowledge.

How deeply we are all immersed in the world of duality is clear in the bewilderment we must all share through our Western conditioning in the matter of 'inner' and 'outer'. Blake was very clear in his understanding that the externalization of nature is a tragic consequence of what he called the 'wrenching apart' of the apparently external world from the unity of the wholeness of being. This has created an unhealed wound in the soul of modern Western man, leaving nature soulless and lifeless, and the inner world abstracted from the natural universe, its proper home. In the *unus mundus* the very terms 'inner' and 'outer' are not applicable at all. Both soul and nature have suffered; nature by being banished, in Blake's words, 'outside existence' in 'a soul-shuddering vacuum', natural space. At the same time the soul can no longer inhabit nature, and the 'afterlife' is situated—again in Blake's words— 'in an allegoric abode where existence has never come'. But, for the universal spiritual teaching, mind is not in space, but space in mind. 'Nothing', as it is said in the *Hermetica*, 'is more capacious than the incorporeal.'

It is hard to reverse the more or less unconscious assumptions of a culture, and to turn our heads, like the prisoners in Plato's Cave who had taken the shadows of things for realities and were at first dazzled and bewildered by the light. But such

a reversal—and more and more leading scientists are themselves coming to think so—the times demand, not of a learned
few but of the world as a whole. Science itself has come full
circle to this confrontation with the observing mind as an element in the phenomena observed. Many can see clearly, and
many more obscurely feel, that some essential thing is lacking in our ways of life and thought. We have reached this
confrontation; and I believe a change of the premises of our
civilization is about to take place, that naïve realism is already
an obsolete hypothesis. Nothing in history is static and we are
moved by invisible powers, call these what we will.

What is only now dawning on the Western mind was
already plain to Blake, when he wrote:

> in your own Bosom you bear your Heaven
> And Earth & all you behold; tho' it appears Without,
> it is Within,
> In your Imagination, of which this World of Mortality
> is but a Shadow.

A shadow, an image in a mirror; 'for now we see through a
glass, darkly, but then face to face'.

'Matter' is in any case—and this the scientists themselves
have taught us—such a mysterious and insubstantial thing, if
it exists, as such, at all. That stone Dr Johnson kicked seemed
to him real and solid enough when he said with such naïve
assurance (referring to Berkeley, who held the same view as
Blake and the Neoplatonists and the *Hermetica*), 'thus I refute
him'. All those spinning fields of force the scientists tell us of
seem far from Dr Johnson's stone, and much nearer to 'matter'
as Plotinus understood it, as a shadowy *non-ens* which, the
more we pursue, the more it recedes into its 'labyrinths' of
mystery. No one knows what matter is in its ultimate nature.
Stones were quite solid for Berkeley also, and tulips quite real,

but for different reasons: because he saw them. And we too have to realize, in Yeats's words (referring to Berkeley):

> That this pragmatical, preposterous pig of a world, its
> farrow that so solid seem,
> Must vanish on the instant, did the mind but change
> its theme.

Of course consciousness cannot be transformed by a mere change of opinion; rather it involves a change of our whole receptivity, an opening of the heart, the senses and the imagination. Consciousness is in the Vedantic writings described as synonymous with being, and being with bliss: *sat-chit-ananda.* Bliss is a word Blake also used, and he too associated it with the principle of life itself:

> And trees & birds & beasts & men behold their eternal joy.
> Arise, you little glancing wings, and sing your infant joy!
> Arise, and drink your bliss, for every thing that lives is holy!

Plotinus writes of 'felicity' as proper to all living beings, animals and plants no less than humanity, when these attain the fullness of their development, as a plant expands in the sun. Consciousness and nature are not two separate orders, but one and indivisible; to know this, to experience this, is to heal the divided consciousness, in modern jargon the 'schizophrenia' of modern secular thought, which since the Renaissance has grown ever deeper. It is to restore a lost wholeness, the *unus mundus,* that unity of inner and outer, nature and the soul, sought by the alchemists. It is the secret that can transform crude matter into the gold of the 'philosopher's stone', into something of infinite value.

Is it not, besides, an experience very familiar to us, for in childhood did we not know instinctively the values and meanings of all we saw? Can we not all remember a time when not only did we talk to animals and birds and plants and stones and stars and sun and moon, but they to us? C. S. Lewis in his Narnia children's books writes of 'talking animals', who communicate meaning, not perhaps in words, but none the less clearly and unmistakably. One of the distastrous consequences, as Blake saw it, of the materialist philosophy is that we could no longer communicate with the things of nature:

> a Rock, a Cloud, a Mountain
> Were now not Vocal as in Climes of happy Eternity
> Where the lamb replies to the infant voice, & the lion to
>   the man of years
> Giving them sweet instructions; where the Cloud, the
>   River & the Field
> Talk with the husbandman & shepherd.

The natural world 'wanders away' into the 'far remote', and the animals 'build a habitation separate from man'. 'The stars flee remote . . . and all the mountains and hills shrink up like a withering gourd.' These are not changes in the object but in the consciousness of the perceiver.

Blake addresses one of the four sections of his last great prophetic book, *Jerusalem*, 'To the Jews' and appeals to the Jewish esoteric tradition of the primordial man, Adam Kadmon, when he writes:

> You have a tradition, that Man anciently contain'd in his mighty limbs all things in Heaven and Earth: this you received from the Druids.
>
> 'But now the Starry Heavens are fled from the mighty limbs of Albion.'

— the Giant Albion, who is the English national being: we are Albion.

To those unaccustomed to the symbolic language in which alone it is possible to speak of invisible realities this may seem remote from anything that can concern us today. In fact this is by no means so, and the esoteric teaching that 'Man anciently contain'd in his mighty limbs all things in Heaven and Earth' is perhaps only now becoming comprehensible in terms other than mythological. Blake, here as throughout his writings, is taking issue with the materialist philosophy that separates all things in heaven and earth from the 'body' of man.

Let us examine what he is in reality saying. The human 'body' as Blake uses the term is much more than the physical frame, to which indeed Blake always refers as 'the garment not the man'. In this respect he is following Swedenborg, his earliest master, who is himself drawing on that primordial tradition to which Blake refers. Plato wrote that 'the true man' is intellect; Blake changed the term to 'imagination', which he called 'the true man'. Under either term the meaning is that man is not merely his physical but his mental and spiritual being. According to Swedenborg this human 'body' is neither large nor small, not being in space at all; it is a spiritual and mental body which is not contained in the material universe. Mind is not in space, but space in mind, which contains the entire universe that we see, hear, touch and know. This 'body' Swedenborg called the 'Divine Humanity', a phrase most of us associate rather with Blake, who borrowed it, and identified the term (as did Swedenborg) with the Eternal Christ, Blake's 'Jesus, the Imagination'. 'This world of Imagination is the world of Eternity,' Blake writes. 'All Things are comprehended in their Eternal Forms in the divine body of the Saviour, the True Vine of Eternity, the Human Imagination.' 'I am the true vine,' Jesus says; 'I am the vine, ye are the branches'; and so the mystics have ever understood his words. All humanity is incorporated within this great spiritual organism; not a mechanism, but being, living and conscious, a 'person', whom Swedenborg described as 'the Grand Man of the Heavens', the collective spiritual being of all humanity.

Some of you may here recall Plato's parable of the first human beings, who were spherical. And it seems that this was more than a joke by Aristophanes at the banquet; for is not the universe of the scientists said to be spherical because of the curvature of the path of light? And is not each of us, in this sense, the centre of a spherical universe which 'contains all things in heaven and earth'? And as all see the same sun, so from our myriad centres we each contain not a part of the universe but the whole. It is this tradition—the primordial tradition of that first religion of all humanity that Blake attributes, rightly or wrongly, to 'the Druids', that Blake in his address 'To the Jews' recalls. In symbolic terms the Jewish Adam Kadmon, humanity as first created 'in the image of God', is the same as Blake's and Swedenborg's 'Divine Humanity', and the Christian's mystical body of Christ present in and to every created human individual. Man in reality still contains in his mighty limbs all things in heaven and earth but through the 'wrenching apart' of inner and outer worlds, the 'mortal worm', the 'worm of sixty winters' has lost his spiritual body and his universe is all outside him. It is through the materialist philosophy that modern man has come to this pass, summed up in Blake's line: 'But now the Starry Heavens are fled from the mighty limbs of Albion.' Albion is the English nation, and it is in England that Bacon, Newton and Locke (whom Blake holds responsible for the 'wrenching apart') elaborated the materialist system which has since overspread the whole world. (There was of course also Descartes, but Blake was an Englishman.) The 'starry heavens' are Newton's especial domain; and by, as Blake understood the matter, separating the stars from the mountains, the mountains from man, and postulating a space–time universe outside mind itself, man becomes only 'a little grovelling root outside of himself', and the physical body, which is in reality only a 'form and organ' of boundless life, seems all. How differently the world appears when the rift between man and his universe is healed, Blake has sought to express in the poem 'Milton', whose theme is the world of Imagination. Answering Newton, for whom space is an external system, Blake writes of the same universe seen as being within the human imagination. 'The Sky is an Immortal Tent', he wrote:

And every Space that a Man views around his dwelling-place
Standing on his own roof or in his garden on a mount
Of twenty-five cubits in height, such space is his Universe:
And on its verge the sun rises & sets, the Clouds bow
To meet the flat Earth & the Sea in such an order'd Space:
The Starry heavens reach on further, but here bend and set
On all sides, & the two Poles turn on their valves of gold:
And if he move his dwelling-place, his heavens also move
Where'er he goes, and all his neighbourhood bewail his loss.
Such are the Spaces called Earth & such its dimension.

Spaces are, according to Blake, 'visionary', and time and space come into being by the creative power of the imagination, measured out 'to mortal man every morning'. For him it is all so very simple, not at all because he took issue with Newton on the 'facts' or arguments of his system (which within its own terms is not to be faulted) but because his premisses were quite other.

Teilhard de Chardin has made an attempt to situate the theory of evolution within a spiritual rather than a materialist context; the divine humanity (to use Blake's term) is implicit in the alpha, to emerge as the omega of creation by the One who says, 'I am alpha and omega, the first and the last.' Naïve materialism must deem man an accident in a blind mechanism. Somehow the less can produce the greater by the laws of chance. Was it Bertrand Russell who calculated the chances of a thousand monkeys at a thousand typewriters producing the plays of Shakespeare? Absurd as the notion is, it is a calculation that has to be made by those who deny spiritual cause. It seems self-evident that a mechanism cannot produce spirit; but spirit can embody itself. The greater can produce the less, but the less cannot produce the greater, nor can the laws of chance write the plays of Shakespeare, who could write, on this very subject,

> What a piece of work is a man, how noble in reason, how infinite in faculties, in form and moving, how express and admirable in action, how like an angel in apprehension, how like a god: the beauty of the world; the paragon of animals; and yet to me, what is this quintessence of dust?

Can dust of itself produce such a quintessence? The materialist would have it so; and Blake, with his genius for going to the heart of things, saw no third alternative: 'Man is either the ark of God or a phantom of the earth and of the water.' If the naïve materialist supposes that 'nature' can produce man, that man is a product of nature, sacred tradition sees, on the contrary, 'nature' as the domain of man.

Blake insisted continually on the 'human' character of the natural world, in its whole and in its parts; for 'nature' *is* the human imagination when understood not as a mechanism but as a 'vision', a reflection of the one living and indivisible universe.

> Each grain of Sand,
> Every Stone on the Land,

> Each rock & each hill,
> Each fountain & rill,
> Each herb & each tree,
> Mountain, hill, earth & sea,
> Cloud, Meteor & Star
> Are Men Seen Afar.

'All is Human, Mighty, Divine,' he wrote; not in an excess of emotion but with the certitude of a profound understanding.

Swedenborg—who as we have seen was in the eighteenth century the principal defender of this mode of thought—elaborated his famous theory of 'correspondences'. If every creature is seen as the 'correspondence' of its inner nature—for such is Swedenborg's teaching—we find in the outer world continually and everywhere, in beasts and birds down to the minutest insects, the expression of 'spirits of different orders and capacities' whose outer forms bear the imprint of their living natures. Swedenborg was by profession a scientist (he was Assessor of Minerals to the Swedish Government) and his pages on the rich variety of living creatures, understood as 'correspondences' of states of being, certainly inspired Blake, who in his battle against materialism does not fail to make use of this view of nature as an expression of the living Imagination. He too presents the creatures not as objects but as forms of life:

> Does the whale worship at thy footsteps as the hungry dog;
> Or does he scent the mountain prey because his nostrils
>   wide
> Draw in the ocean? does his eye discern the flying cloud
> As the raven's eye? or does he measure the expanse like
>   the vulture?
> Does the still spider view the cliffs where eagles hide their
>   young;

Or does the fly rejoice because the harvest is brought in?
Does not the eagle scorn the earth & despise the treasures
   beneath?
But the mole knoweth what is there, & the worm shall
   tell it thee.
Does not the worm erect a pillar in the mouldering
   church yard
And a palace of eternity in the jaws of the hungry grave?

Everything in nature has its inner no less than its outer being.
The 'mortal worm' is 'translucent all within' and of 'the little
winged fly smaller than a grain of sand', Blake writes:

It has a heart like thee, a brain open to heaven & hell,
Withinside wondrous & expansive; its gates are not
   clos'd:
I hope thine are not: hence it clothes itself in rich array:
Hence thou art cloth'd with human beauty, O thou
   mortal man.

Yet another version of the figure of the Universal Man who
contains in himself all things—Blake's Divine Humanity,
the Imagination, is the One distributed in the Many, like the
Egyptian God Osiris, scattered throughout the universe,
whose 'body' is reassembled by the devotion of his wife Isis:

So man looks out in tree & herb & fish & bird & beast
Collecting up the scatter'd portions of his immortal body
Into the Elemental forms of every thing that grows.
   . . .
In pain he sighs, in pain he labours in his universe,
Screaming in birds over the deep, & howling in the wolf
Over the slain, & moaning in the cattle, & in the winds
                                        . . . his voice
Is heard throughout the Universe: wherever a grass grows

Or a leaf buds, The Eternal Man is seen, is heard, is felt,
And all his sorrows, till he reassumes his ancient bliss.

Blake is following the Swedenborgian doctrine of 'correspondences'which is, of course, a continuation of the earlier
alchemical and astrological doctrine of 'signatures'. Everything in nature, according to this prematerialist view, bears in
its outer form the 'signature' of its qualities. Plants, animals,
minerals are classified according to their qualities by an elab-
orate system of 'signatures' from planets and the houses of
the Zodiac, themselves deemed to be under the guidance of
heavenly influences. Albeit modern thought has discarded the
literal interpretation of these influences as coming from 'the
stars' or planets in a physical sense, nevertheless this older
cosmology can be understood as a projection of the Imagination into the natural universe, a model of the *unus mundus*
which affirms the intrinsic qualities and order of the visible
world. Applied to human nature astrological correspondences
similarly describe and affirm the unity of inner and outer, man
the microcosm within the macrocosm of the universe. Or, as
Blake and Swedenborg would have it, the outer universe is
within man. Dismissed as an inexact and rudimentary science,
are we not now obliged to re-examine alchemy, astrology and
the rest—as C. G. Jung has done—as pertaining rather to our
inner universe, and to the indivisibility of inner and outer? As
the alchemists, and before them the Neoplatonists understood,
'nature' is a mirror, a looking-glass in which we see reflected
everything that is, and everything we are. We are once more in
a living universe, a universe moreover whose life is not alien to
us but indistinguishable, inseparable, part and parcel of what
we ourselves are. This, it seems to me, is the point at which we,
at this time, are; where human knowledge has brought us. I
suggest that we are not in a phase of further development of

materialist science in directions already foreseeable, but at the moment of a reversal of premises, a change of direction. Not, indeed, that anything of the scientific observation of the natural phenomena will be denied or invalidated; science in the modern sense is one of the ways of observing the world, nor is it necessary in order to study what Owen Barfield many years ago named the 'appearances' to accept the materialist standpoint. The greater knowledge does not invalidate the partial, but can include it. It is the claim of the natural sciences to be that all-inclusive knowledge that is no longer tenable.

Would such a change—will such a change—or dare I say, *is* such a change—a venture into a new and unknown experience, or is it not rather something already familiar, which in our heart of hearts we already know? There have been societies, indeed civilizations, where the unity and wholeness of being which our own has gradually lost, has been understood by the wise and the simple alike. Blake supposes it to be man's primordial condition to contain in his mighty limbs all things in heaven and earth. Have we not all read Laurens van der Post's poignant accounts of the doomed African Bushmen whose physical survival was precarious indeed, but who felt themselves, so he tells us, to be perfectly at one with their world, because nothing in that world was alien to them, nothing without meaning? I quote from his latest book *Testament to the Bushmen:*

> The essence of this being, I believe, was his sense of belonging: belonging to nature, the universe, life and his own humanity. He had committed himself utterly to nature as a fish to the sea. He had no sense whatsoever of property, owned no animals and cultivated no land. Life and nature owned all and he accepted without question that,

provided he was obedient to the urge of the world within him, the world without, which was not separate in his spirit, would provide. How right he was is proved by the fact that nature was kinder to him by far than civilization ever was. This feeling of belonging set him apart from us on the far side of the deepest divide in the human spirit.

And Laurens van der Post goes on to write:

> We were rich and powerful where he was poor and vulnerable: he was rich where we were poor and his spirit led to strange water for which we secretly longed. But, above all, he came into our estranged and divided vision, confident in his belonging and clothed as brightly as Joseph's coat of dream colours in his own unique experience of life.

Above all the Bushman experienced always 'the feeling of being known'. And the author confesses that he himself experienced an overwhelming sense of nostalgia

> for this shining sense of belonging, of being known and possessing a cosmic identity of one's own, recognized by all from insect to sun, moon and stars which kept him company, so that he felt he had the power to influence them as they influenced and helped him.

Earth was not only the Bushmen's home, source of material nourishment and shelter, but also of their spiritual food. The earth is full of meaning; tells them those marvellous stories of Mantis and the Lynx and the Morning Star, of lizard and beetle and wild freesia, living in their rich and manifold lives some one or other aspect of the world's one and indivisible being. As Blake says, earth would 'talk' with the husbandman and the shepherd.

With this imaginative apprehension goes always a sense of

the sacred. But where are the holy places of the modern technological world? And do we need holy places, all those sacred springs and wells and rivers and trees and anthills and caverns and mountains where the gods live? I would reply that, since we have the capacity to experience awe and wonder and love, these are within the range of human experience without whose use we are diminished, as by blindness or deafness. Modern secular man finds no burning bush, no Presence which commands, 'put off thy shoes from off thy feet, for the place whereon thou standest is holy ground'. But in losing the capacity for awe, for wonder, for the sense of the numinous, the sacred, what we lose is not the object but that part of ourselves which can find in tree or churinga-stone or the dread cavern of the pythoness the correspondence of an aspect of our humanity of which these are the objective correlative, the correspondence, the mirror, the 'signature'. The Presence that spoke to Moses from the Burning Bush speaks on in every age: 'I AM THAT I AM.' A mystery insoluble!

We will never, certainly—nor should we wish to do so—return to the innocent world of the Stone Age. We can never un-know what the scientific investigation of nature has presented to us. It has described in the minutest detail and the grandest scope that image in the 'vegetable glass of nature'. But until we have experienced the unity of all things not as a natural fact but as a living presence we shall never, in the early mystic Traherne's words, know the world 'aright'.

What this learned and cultured divine has written re-echoes down the ages from the Stone Age to ourselves:

You never Enjoy the World aright, till the Sea itself floweth in your Veins, till you are Clothed with the Heavens, and Crowned with the Stars: and Perceiv your self to be the Sole Heir of the whole World: and more . . . becaus Men are in

it who are evry one of Sole Heirs, as well as you . . . Till
your Spirit fills the whole World, and the Stars are your
Jewels.

It is the part of the poet to present to us that total view and experience of reality which includes all aspects of our humanity
in the context of every age. Or that situates every age, rather,
in the context of the everlasting. Such poets have, even so,
written in this century—I think of Valéry and Claudel, of
Rilke and of Yeats, indeed of T. S. Eliot and of Edwin Muir
and Vernon Watkins, of Robert Frost—and there are others
less complete or less illustrious. I know no poetry that goes
beyond that of Rilke in stating—suggesting rather—who we
are, what our place is in the universe. Rainer Maria Rilke, near
the end of his life, in a brief period of continuous and prophetic inspiration, completed his two greatest poetic works,
the *Duino Elegies* and the *Sonnets to Orpheus*. Rejecting institu-
tionalized religion he was the more free to experience those
'angels', intelligences of the universe, 'beyond the stars'. What
are we, he asks, beside these great transhuman orders? And he
replies:

> Praise this world to the Angel, not the untellable; you
> can't impress him with the splendour you've felt; in the
>   cosmos
> where he more feelingly feels you're only a novice. So
>   show him
> some simple thing, refashioned by age after age
> till it lives in our hands and eyes as a part of ourselves.
> Tell him *things* . . ..

To the things of this earth it is mankind who gives their
reality. It is these only we can tell the Angel:

> Above all, the hardness of life,
> The long experience of love, in fact
> purely untellable things. But later,
> under the stars, what use? the more deeply untellable stars?
> For the wanderer too doesn't bring from mountain
>   to valley
> a handful of earth, for all untellable earth, but only
> a word he has won, pure, the yellow and blue
> gentian. Are we, perhaps, *here* just for saying: House,
> Bridge, Fountain, Gate, Jug, Fruit-tree, Window –
> possibly: Pillar, Tower? . . ..

It is we who give meaning to these things by our words, by performing Adam's appointed task of 'naming' the creation. Thus we bestow on the creatures not a merely natural, but a human, an imaginative and invisible reality. And Rilke continues his thought that we are here 'just for saying' the names:

> but for *saying*, remember,
> oh, for such saying as never the things themselves
> hoped so intensely to be. Is not the secret purpose
> of this sly Earth, in urging a pair of lovers,
> just to make everything leap with ecstasy in them?

The world finds in us an intenser, a totally new mode of being; as if we are here to perform an alchemical transmutation of crude base 'nature' into the gold of Imagination. And to the Angel we can show 'how happy a thing can be, how guileless and ours'; even in its transience:

> These things that live on departure
> understand when you praise them: fleeting, they look for
> rescue through something in us, the most fleeting of all.
> Want us to change them entirely, within our invisible hearts
> into—oh, endlessly—into ourselves! Whosoever we are.

Whosoever we are. That is a mystery which we cannot in our very nature hope to resolve. It has been the *hubris* of science to hope to know everything. The poet, more humble, seeks to discern who and what we are within a totality greater than ourselves, a finally unknowable order. We are nevertheless the custodians and creators of that order of values and realities that are properly human, that human kingdom of the Imagination 'ever expanding in the bosom of God'. That 'divine body', the human Imagination, is the underlying order which bounds, embraces and contains the human universe.

Within the tradition of spiritual knowledge which I have indicated, the underlying order is not some system of natural laws but being itself, at once the 'person' and the 'place' of the universe. Within this whole we are, in our present state, aware only of the limited field of our own lives. We are aware of other lives, and great fields beyond us, other times and places and being and modes of being surrounding us like unexplored forests or unclimbed mountains or unsailed seas. A sort of fragrance, or music, is sometimes borne to us on an invisible wind from those far-off fields of knowledge and experience, and we wish we could experience more of that whole of which each of us is at once an infinitesimal part and an infinite centre.

At the British Museum recently I walked from one exhibit to another in an exhibition of Buddhist scriptures, devotedly and minutely transcribed in languages unknown to most of those who visited that exhibition, on tablets of wood or pages of palm-leaves, by forgotten monks whose days were spent in meditating the truths of a great civilization that rose like a tide over the Eastern world, to ebb again, and whose records end in a museum as in an honoured grave. And before, the unwritten knowledge and unrecorded visions of civilizations still more remote. And again beyond the vast regions of the once known and the knowable, that given an infinite number

of lifetimes—perhaps that very infinite number of which
there are, or have been or will be, human lives—there may be
other beings attuned not to the spectrum of our human senses
but to other, ampler magnitudes. In every hedgerow are there
not minute lives of birds and bees and insects, whose worlds
are to us impenetrable? Within us something seems to discern
an underlying order, a unity of being, 'the One' of which Plato
wrote, the All, the God Itself. Or, as the subtler, deeper wisdom of India in the Creation Hymn of the *Rig Veda* takes us to
the extreme limit of the known and the knowable:

> But, after all, who knows, and who can say
>   whence it all came, and how creation happened?
> The gods themselves are later than creation,
>   so who knows truly whence it has arisen?

> Whence all creation had its origin,
>   he, whether he fashioned it or whether he did not,
> he, who surveys it all from highest heaven,
>   he knows – or maybe even he does not know.

⁋ A Sense of Beauty

The materialist ideologies which have for so long prevailed in
the Western world do not speak of beauty, or hold what they
take beauty to be in a low regard as the superficial decoration
of some plain surface or structure, or as synonymous with the
physically desirable and therefore an adjunct to some utility—
typically the beauty of woman as serving the purposes of the
sex instinct; although it could be the apple that beguiled her,
'good for food' and 'pleasant to the eyes'. Both these may
indeed be beautiful although, for those who do not share the
utilitarian values of materialism, for different reasons. For
those who see our true humanity as spiritual in nature beauty
has no utility: rather it belongs to that order of values utility
serves, or ought to serve. At a time when a Reith Lecturer finds
it necessary to waste six lectures in arguing that computers,
although they store information, do not have minds, the con-
fusion of values, not to say the exclusion of values, has surely
reached its point of absurdity. We all know how this has come
about—how, whether we choose to see the beginning of the
process with Bacon, with Descartes, or farther back, with
Aristotle—the now practically universal habit of equating
'reality' with the material order, and 'nature' with material
objects existing in a space–time external to and independent of
mind has come to be seen as self-evident. Yeats wrote of mind
becoming, in the post-Renaissance world, 'passive before a
mechanized nature'. The study of this externalized nature,
'natural science' properly speaking but nowadays simply called
'science' as if there were no other knowledge, prides itself on
its objectivity, its impersonality, its freedom from what are

pejoratively called 'value judgements'. Thus values have in themselves come to be devalued in terms of our dominant mode of evaluation.

A nice instance of this is the case of the French pheno-menologist, Gaston Bachelard, who, as a historian of science, set himself to purge the vocabulary of science of all qualitative terms (gender, elements 'attracting' or 'attacking' one another and the like) only to discover that in his discarded residue of unscientific terms lay a wide range of responses to nature of a different—a qualitative—kind. Bachelard experienced a kind of conversion, following which he wrote his famous books on the four 'elements' in their qualitative nature—*L'eau et les Rêves, L'air et les Songes,* and the rest—wherein he considers nature as a qualitative experience, an ever-living mirror of states of mind.

The exclusion of 'value judgements' in chemical experi-ments is no doubt in some cases at least appropriate, but the habit has spread into other fields, economic, sociological, and nowadays psychological and therefore also moral as well. These fields are subjected to statistical and other scientific or pseudo-scientific 'evaluation' so called; with dire results which would be considered very funny in a sane society, but whose consequences in our own are more often tragic. A Cambridge friend of mine recently told me that a candidate she was examining in a field involving the history of ideas was refused her doctorate by the co-examiner (an American woman) on the grounds that the candidate had included 'judgemental statements'! Such are the consequences—we could all think of instances, but why go on—of the fallacy of 'behaviourism', itself the *reductio ad absurdum* of regarding the universe as a mechanism. Because the mind, the spirit, cannot be quantified it is deemed virtually non-existent, or a mere factor of poten-tial error to be carefully excluded or removed from some statistical report on the 'facts' of history, of human behaviour, of being itself. Thus, for the majority opinion which dominates our English-speaking West, qualities and values are deliberately excluded, or marginalized. Ingenuity and skill we may see everywhere in our world of machines but where do we find beauty?

Sickened by it, David Jones wrote down his own heart's cry: 'A, a, a, Domine Deus'.

I said, Ah! what shall I write?
I enquired up and down.
              (He's tricked me before
with his manifold lurking-places.)
I looked for His symbol at the door.
I have looked for a long while
              at the textures and contours.
I have run a hand over the trivial intersections.
I have journeyed among the dead forms
causation projects from pillar to pylon.
I have tired the eyes of the mind
              regarding the colours and lights.
I have felt for His Wounds
              in nozzles and containers.
I have wondered for the automatic devices.
I have tested the inane patterns
              without prejudice.
I have been on my guard
              not to condemn the unfamiliar.
For it is easy to miss Him
              at the turn of a civilization.
    I have watched the wheels go round in case I might see the living creatures like the appearance of lamps, in case I might see the Living God projected from the Machine. I have said

to the perfected steel, be my sister and for the glassy towers I thought I felt some beginnings of His creature, but *A, a, a, Domine Deus,* my hands found the glazed work unrefined and the terrible crystal a stage-paste . . . *Eia, Domine Deus.*

The world of machines that our civilization has made in the image of a mechanistic ideology is terrible because without qualities, because it has fallen to the point at which men and women have come to regard themselves as machines and to attribute to their machines knowledge: an idolatry unprecedented. David Jones looked in the machine in vain for 'the Living God'; and above all for 'his wounds'; it being in our capacity to be wounded, to suffer and to love that humanity lies and also divinity. One might contrast 'A, a, a, Domine Deus' with Blake's poem 'The Divine Image' addressed 'To Mercy, Pity, Peace, and Love', an image both divine and human. Computers can store facts, television sets can communicate them, but no machine is capable of mercy, pity, peace and love. Perhaps it is precisely in those things that cannot be mechanized that our humanity lies—in the excluded realm of values, immeasurable, imponderable, and for ever eluding quantification.

Beauty is of course something that many—even many scientists—do find everywhere expressed in 'nature'. Indeed it is that very beauty that must have attracted these scientists to the study of the vast and the minute forms of nature, plant morphology, crystals, animal and plant metamorphoses, the interior structures and transformations of living cells or inorganic particles. It would be less than human not to see beauty in snow crystals, the night sky, the ripples and waves of water, the whole marvellous epiphany we daily behold.

Beauty is immeasurable because it is an experience of the mind or spirit and has no quantifiable reality at all; although attempts have been made to discover those proportions, both in architecture and in the human form (and other natural forms) that can be regarded as the measures of beauty. Such is the harmony that exists between 'nature' and the perceiving mind that such proportions and forms no doubt do exist and are universally acknowledged in music, in architecture, in anatomy. Yet is still remains true that 'beauty is in the eye of the beholder'—a truism but also a truth. Once we transfer our attention from the object—nature—to the perceiving mind, a whole new range of considerations appears. Instead of asking, what in nature should be considered beautiful, we must ask what in us enables us to perceive beauty?

First we must dismiss the notion that mind is a passive recipient of sense impressions from a great inhuman external mechanism; an outer world which all see alike but about which we may form different judgements, draw different conclusions, more or less true according to our 'objectivity'—the great scientific virtue so misapplied when the arts are in question. We, on the contrary, are extremely variable, not only because of our great differences between one and another, but in ourselves, from youth to age, from day to day, from mood to mood. Our minds are by no means passive recipients of impressions, but continually active, in actually creating what we see, hear, experience, know; for what we experience is knowledge. One might even say that since knowledge is an experience, by that very definition whatever can be stored in a computer is by that very fact not 'knowledge' at all.

Beauty, understood as an experience and not as a quality in objects, is by no means a common measure like the golden section, or the anatomical proportions followed by the Renaissance painters and sculptors or by Indian makers of images. Doubtless, almost magical correlations could be found between these proportions and the perceiving mind; but in another sense beauty is an aspect that absolutely anything in the world may assume when seen in a certain way. We, it is true, live in a drab world, and the 'kitchen sink' is a phrase describing a recent school of drama and writing which sought to express that drabness in a spirit somewhere between protest and self-pity. David Gascoyne recently described (in conversation) the prevailing theme of most contemporary verse, the majority point of view, as 'the celebration of the commonplace'—the celebration, that is, of commonplaceness as such; and without very much in the way of either social protest or self-pity, more in the spirit of simply seeing things as they are, with perhaps a note of self-congratulation for honesty. Little place for beauty here, nor is the word nor the concept invoked, rather deliberately banished as dishonest escapism. The commonplace overspreads nature too (dead fish, polluted rivers, joyless birds) and this reductionism as applied to nature is nowadays very popular.

All this passed through my mind after visiting the 1984 exhibition of Vermeer and other seventeenth-century Dutch painters at Burlington House.

Many—one might say most—of these have chosen for their theme the commonplace, many the kitchen sink itself— women preparing food, sweeping the floor, pouring wine, going about the simple tasks of life, unhurried. In all there was a certain joy in these things, in Vermeer himself, simple human life was (to use Wordsworth's phrase) 'apparelled in celestial light'; plain women, ordinary men, tables, windows, small rooms, the commonplace, was enveloped in beauty. Why, wherein the difference?

True, the commonplace things that were in daily use in Vermeer's world were made by craftsmen, with a certain quality that machine-made mass-produced objects lack; the modern kitchen sink is made of pressed steel or plastic and so are many of the things we use in everyday life; they have the anonymity, the impersonality, the inhuman imprint of the machine. But it is more than that, and in any case after a little use any object takes on the character of the user. One can say, besides, that not all painters of the seventeenth century saw their world apparelled in celestial light; Jan Steen seldom rises above a tolerant and earthy commonplace, certainly he does not attain to that mysterious quality of beauty. Nor is it any mere skill in the use of paint (people are for ever telling one how well Francis Bacon handles paint, as no doubt he does) but lies in a difference in the way the painter sees the world. Could we say that Vermeer saw with the eyes of love? Of a certain kind of love that discerns the spiritual mystery inherent in those people, even those things, which he paints? Is the secret of beauty perhaps that only love can behold it? And what is love? Again, it is a human gift that cannot be quantified or measured. It was not that Vermeer was *in* love with those quiet Dutch housewives, mothers and daughters who tend the shrines of life—no, but he saw who they were in the light not of a materialist ideology, but in the light of eternity, of a scale of values of the imagination. Can we say that beauty is the aspect of things loved?

It can happen in any century; and whatever beauty might be found in the commonplace objects of seventeenth-century Holland was certainly not to be found in the lower middle-class kitchen of twentieth-century Dublin of which James Joyce wrote in his *Portrait of the Artist as a Young Man*. In the following passage he is writing with nostalgia of the home and the religious faith he was about to leave, but saw in retrospect as he had seen it once. In the simplicity of love. He is writing of the end of his adolescence when home and religion still held him; shaken into penitence at a school retreat (the sermons of the Jesuit are re-created with brilliant mockery) he went to confession before returning home:

> He knelt to say his penance, praying in a corner of the dark nave; and his prayers ascended to heaven from his purified heart like perfume streaming upwards from a heart of white rose.
>
> The muddy streets were gay. He strode homeward, conscious of an invisible grace pervading and making light his limbs. In spite of all he had done it. He had confessed and God had pardoned him. His soul was made fair and holy once more, holy and happy.
> . . .
> He sat by the fire in the kitchen, not daring to speak for happiness. Till that moment he had not known how beautiful and peaceful life could be. The green square of paper pinned round the lamp cast down a tender shade. On the dresser was a plate of sausages and white pudding and on the shelf there were eggs. They would be for the breakfast in the morning after the communion in the college chapel. White pudding and eggs and sausages and cups of tea. How simple and beautiful was life after all! And life lay all before him.

'The green square of paper round the lamp cast down a tender shade'—the touch is worthy of Vermeer and the light— or 'tender shade'—is the same, it is the light of love.

The word love, like the word beauty, is one not in current use; the materialist equivalent is 'sex', a physiological word, not at all the same thing, though sex also can be apparelled in celestial light. But love is that vision of transfiguration which unveils the beauty not of people only but of everything in

the world. Blake, matter of fact as always when speaking of
heavenly things, speaks neither of beauty nor of love but of
that transforming vision itself: 'A fool sees not the same tree
that a wise man sees', and against the consensus of opinion
that sees the world as drab or commonplace. To Dr Trusler
he wrote:

> I feel that a Man may be happy in This World. And I know
> that This World Is a World of imagination & Vision. I see
> Every thing I paint In This World, but Every body does not
> see alike. To the Eyes of a Miser a Guinea is more beautiful
> than the Sun, & a bag worn with the use of Money has
> more beautiful proportions than a Vine filled with Grapes.
> The tree which moves some to tears of joy is in the Eyes of
> others only a green thing that stands in the way. Some See
> Nature all Ridicule & Deformity, & by these I shall not
> regulate my proportions; & Some Scarce see Nature at all.
> But to the Eyes of the Man of Imagination, Nature is Imagi-
> nation itself. As a man is, So he Sees. As the Eye is formed,
> such are its Powers. You certainly Mistake, when you say
> that the Visions of Fancy are not to be found in This World.
> To Me This World is all One continued Vision of Fancy or
> Imagination . . . .

Wordsworth, as we know, associated that vision of the
beauty of the world with childhood, something inevitably lost
with the years; the opening lines of his Ode 'On Intimations
of Immortality from Recollections of early childhood' express
a whole doctrine (Platonic or Neoplatonic in essence) of the
descent of the soul from an eternal world, accompanied by a
forgetting:

> The Soul that rises with us, or life's star
> Hath had elsewhere its setting,

> And cometh from afar:
> Not in entire forgetfulness,
> And not in utter nakedness,
> But trailing clouds of glory do we come . . ..

But the years dim this vision:

> There was a time when meadow, grove, and stream,
> The earth, and every common sight,
>   To me did seem
> Apparelled in celestial light,
> The glory and the freshness of a dream.
> It is not now as it hath been of yore; –
> Turn wheresoe'er I may,
>   By night or day
>   The things which I have seen I now can see no
>   more.

With bitterness the poet felt his loss; 'That there hath passed away a glory from the earth'.

Traherne too, the poet and divine, who died in 1674, found, as Wordsworth did, 'intimations of immortality' in childhood's vision; in the third of his 'Centuries of Meditation' he writes of 'Those Pure and Virgin Apprehensions I had from the Womb, and that Divine Light wherewith I was born . . . . By the Gift of GOD they attended me into the World, and by His Special favor I remember them till now' — and he writes of that vision as no poet before or since:

> All appeared New, and Strange at first, inexpressibly rare and delightful and beautiful. I was a little Stranger which at my Enterance into the World was Saluted and Surrounded with innumerable Joys. My Knowledg was Divine. I knew by Intuition those things which since my Apostasie, I Collected again by the Highest Reason. My very Ignorance was

Advantageous. I seemed as one Brought into the Estate of Innocence. All things were Spotles and Pure and Glorious: yea, and infinitly mine, and Joyful, and Precious . . . . I saw all in the peace of Eden; Heaven and Earth did sing my Creators Praises, and could not make more Melody to Adam, then to me. All Time was Eternity, and a Perpetual Sabbath.

—and the poet goes on to remember:

The Corn was Orient and Immortal Wheat, which never should be reaped, nor was ever sown. I thought it had stood from everlasting to everlasting. The Dust and Stones of the Street were as Precious as GOLD: the Gates were at first the End of the World. The Green Trees when I saw them first through one of the Gates Transported and Ravished me; their Sweetness and unusual Beauty made my Heart to leap, and almost mad with Exstasie; they were such strange and Wonderful Thing. The Men! O what Venerable and reverend Creatures did the Aged seem! Immortal Cherubims! And yong Men Glittering and Sparkling Angels and Maids strange Seraphick Pieces of Life and Beauty! Boys and Girls Tumbling in the street, and Playing, were moving Jewels. I knew not that they were Born or should die. But all things abided Eternaly as they were in their Proper Places . . . .

Traherne was of the century of Vermeer; and it may be that the shadow of the materialist ideology had not then fallen so heavily on the world; yet not all saw the world in that light of eternity; nor in our own century is that vision altogether absent. We have seen that James Joyce caught its fleeting gleam before he turned away; nor can it be said that the present world is far too terrible for it to be even permissible to see this world of terror and violence 'apparell'd in Celestial Light'. For it was a Jew—Marc Chagall—who came from Russia to Paris and who has lived to see the holocaust of his people who has most radiantly captured it. While his Russian contemporaries were caught up in the excitement of the communist revolution, were painting 'structuralist' compositions, abstract and full of acute angles, Chagall, rooted in the Jewish spirituality of his inheritance, was painting a world of poverty and persecution in the celestial light. Traherne wrote that 'Love is the true means by which the World is Enjoyed; Our Lov to others, and Others Lov to us.'

Chagall is full of love; a Rabbi is reading the scripture with such intensity that he does not even notice the tenderness with which his wife is feeding him from a spoon with milk—woman's nourishment on more levels than one. Lovers dream, making their bed in some great bunch of lilac and summer flowers; a Jew prays with such intensity that his head is released from his body on to another plane of being; a bride in her bridal white, a new-born babe still red with the blood of birth; even the crucifixion (the eternal crucifixion of the Jewish race)—all these are poor, obscure, often tragic people, transfigured by love into a beauty that melts the heart. Love is not clever, or experimental, or concerned with those things that preoccupy the avant-garde of all times; rather it is unerringly certain, possessing the secret of discerning beauty where others do not see it. Thousands have understood Van Gogh's chair, a common poor man's chair but painted with a tragic intensity of love.

Or, to come nearer home, there is Stanley Spencer, oddest of visionaries; whose vision survived his years in the army as a private soldier of the First World War. Once I remember he was talking of Cookham, that very ordinary place on the Thames that motorists are more likely to drive through than to stop and admire, which in picture after picture he has painted with an intensity that makes its very ugliness beautiful. Looking at a painting of a certain barn he had done some time before, Stanley had said to himself, 'That is the very essence of Cookham, I will just go and look at it again.' But he could not find the place. The barn was there, but not the place he had seen, for he did not take with him the light in which he had seen it; it had become drab and ordinary. The celestial light had faded. It is only in the light of eternity that we see this world beautified.

Are these privileged moments, then, a matter of mere happy chance, that come and go? A moment of intoxication, physical or emotional, in which we see through rose-coloured spectacles? This is to imply that Vermeer, that Chagall, that Blake, Stanley Spencer and a host of others were deluded when they saw beauty where others do not, that as we grow wiser we see drabness and vulgarity where before we saw the dust and stones of the street as precious gold. Those whom experience has made wise know that dust and stones are not precious or made of gold. Writers of doctorate theses on Blake—especially transatlantic students—copy from one to another the view that, according to Blake, first there is childhood's innocence and the golden vision, but that then we have to 'learn from experience' and see the darkness. Perhaps in the end we can embrace both points of view. Nothing could be more mistaken—for Blake 'experience' was not a learning but a forgetting (and Wordsworth too so presents it), a loss of vision, a narrowing of consciousness, or, as Blake puts it, a falling into the 'deadly sleep' of materialism, to become oblivious to that beauty seen with the eyes of innocence. In *Vala* he wrote, of the Giant Albion (so Blake names the English nation),

Refusing to behold the Divine Image which all behold
And live thereby, he sunk down into a deadly sleep.

The entire theme of Blake's prophetic writings—and above all of his last and also his darkest work, 'Jerusalem'—is the loss and darkening through a turning away from the spiritual source to the materialist ideologies that in Blake's day were already widespread and obliterating the 'Divine Vision'. 'Turning from Universal Love', Blake wrote, Albion's vision darkened and his heart hardened as he refused to see in all things about him:

> the Divine Similitude
> In loves and tears of brothers, sisters, sons, fathers
>   and friends,
> Which if Man ceases to behold, he ceases to exist.

By no means did Blake share Wordsworth's fatalistic attitude towards the fading of the vision, which for him never did fade. Blake saw the darkening of the vision as, essentially, a failure of love; it is a change not in the world but in ourselves. Coleridge experienced the loss of his vision of beauty no less than Wordsworth did but perceived the cause of that loss more profoundly than did Wordsworth, as residing within himself. In his great poem 'Dejection: an Ode' he is addressing the woman he loves but cannot possess. Grief has darkened his vision of beauty; 'A grief without a pang, void, dark and drear':

> All this long eve, so balmy and serene,
> Have I been gazing on the western sky,
>   And its peculiar tint of yellow green:
> And still I gaze – and with how blank an eye.
> And those thin clouds above, in flakes and bars,
> That give away their motion to the stars;
> Those stars that glide behind them or between,
> Now sparkling, now bedimmed, but always seen:
> Yon crescent Moon, as fixed as if it grew

In its own cloudless, starless lake of blue,
I see them all so excellently fair,
I see, not feel, how beautiful they are!

He goes on to address to Sara Hutchinson his realization—
albeit a realization through its loss—that beauty comes from
the soul and not from nature:

O Lady! we receive but what we give
And in our life alone does Nature live:
Ours is her wedding garment, ours her shroud!
    And would we ought behold, of higher worth,
Than that inanimate cold world allowed
To the poor loveless ever-anxious crowd,
    Ah! from the soul itself must issue forth
A light, a glory, a fair luminous cloud
    Enveloping the Earth –
And from the soul itself must there be sent
    A sweet and potent voice, of its own birth,
Of all sweet sounds the life and element!

What follows comes close to the Indian *sat-chit-ananda*,
being-consciousness-bliss, which is the very essence of life
itself:

O pure of heart! thou need'st not ask of me
What this strong music in the soul may be!
What, and wherein it doth exist,
This light, this glory, this fair luminous mist,
This beautiful and beauty-making power.
    Joy, virtuous Lady! Joy that ne'er was given
Save to the pure, and in their purest hour,
Life, and Life's effluence, cloud at once and shower,
Joy, Lady! is the spirit and the power,
Which wedding Nature to us gives in dower

> A new Earth and new Heaven,
> Undreamt of by the sensual and the proud –
> Joy is the sweet voice, Joy the luminous cloud –
> We in ourselves rejoice!
> And thence flows all that charms or ear or sight,
> All melodies the echoes of that voice,
> All colours a suffusion from that light.

Not one of these poets—Wordsworth, Blake, Traherne, Coleridge—fail to see the vision of beauty as the vision of the unclouded pure soul, a vision of reality. Traherne writes, as do all who have experienced it, of seeing the world as a living epiphany:

> Your Enjoyment of the World is never right, till evry Morning you awake in Heaven; see yourself in your Father's Palace: and look upon the Skies the Earth and the Air, as Celestial Joys: having such a Reverend Esteem of all, as if you were among the Angels.

For none of these poets is the beauty of the world illusory; it is rather in a refusal or an inability to see what is before us that illusion lies. Again I quote Traherne:

> The World is a mirror of infinit Beauty, yet no Man sees it. It is a Temple of Majesty yet no man Regards it. It is a Region of Light and Peace, did not men Disquiet it. It is the Paradice of God. It is more to man since he is fall'n then it was before. It is the place of Angels, and the Gate of Heaven.

For those who have so seen the world—and many who are not poets have so seen it— there is no question of self-delusion, or intoxication as the cause of a vision of the beautiful. Nor is it by a mere sentimental preference that Traherne, like Blake and like all others who have 'seen' call this seeing the world 'aright'. Those who would pretend that 'reality' is the 'inanimate cold world' seen by 'the poor loveless ever-anxious crowd' are saying that the less is truer and more real than the greater; which surely cannot be, since the capacity to experience beauty is innate in all, and that to refuse to use that faculty, or to be unable to do so through some injury to the soul (and an ideology may be, as Blake calls materialism, a deadly sickness) is to be less than we are. Blake sees Albion's darkened world of 'experience' as 'the deadly dreams the soul falls into when it leaves Paradise'. It is the Paradisal vision that is an awakening to reality.

This is, I believe all would agree who have known it, a self-authenticating experience. I have only myself known that vision once and I can only say (as many others have said) that this enlargement of consciousness is like an awakening from the ordinary waking state, and accomplished by the realization that I was seeing more, not less, of what was before my eyes: 'So this is what it is really like' was my reflection. Just as when we love we know that we see those we love more, not less, truly than do those who do not love. What I have tried to say is therefore very simple: beauty is the real aspect of things, when seen aright and with the eyes of love.

Let me end with a Jewish Hassidic story—where I read it or who told it to me I cannot remember. The story as I remember it is this. A devout Jewish couple wished to visit a holy Rabbi who, with his wife, lived in great poverty in a tenement in the poorest quarter of the city. They took with them their young son so that later in life he should remember that he had actually met the saintly Rabbi. So they all went, and sat in the poor shabby room of the Rabbi and his wife conversing and listening. As they were on their way home the father asked his little son what he had thought about the Rabbi and his wife;

'They were like our first parents, Adam and Eve', he said. And what, his father went on, did you think about the place where they were living?' And the child replied: 'It was like Paradise.'

II

ℭ John Donne and the Baroque Doubt

It is now for an entire literary generation that the metaphysical poets have seemed to have the clue to our own situation. It is not difficult to see why. For we, probably the most unhappy, and certainly the most torn by conflict, of all the generations since the seventeenth century, have to make a choice, as they had, between the desirable but doomed, and the less desirable but inevitable. To make a choice, or to find a solution. Whether one sees in Baroque art a resolved or an unresolved conflict, a consideration of what that conflict essentially was cannot fail to compel our respect for the intellectual courage, not to say heroism, of the poet John Donne, who among other great figures of the Baroque period felt its full impact, and held in equipoise, even if only for a moment, those forces of change that in a few years transformed the medieval into the modern world.

His was essentially an intellectual heroism—for even the intellectual can have his heroic age, and that is precisely the case of the metaphysical poets. For it is not for being clever or learned that we admire Donne and his school but for their courage in never deluding themselves as to the implications of the two—often more than two—sides to every problem (reflected in the verbal ambiguities characteristic of the metaphysical poets); their refusal to be blinded by emotion to things of the mind; or by reason to things of the heart; to let anything make them forget how much it takes to make a whole man. For 'metaphysical', as has often been pointed out, is a wholly misleading word. Metaphysical poetry is the least abstract, most concrete of all poetry. Thought permeates every emotion, every physical sensation, and our bodies

> are ours, though they are not wee, Wee are
> the intelligences, they the spheares.

('The spheares', that is, in a universe in which, though Copernicus had effected some changes, he had not deposed God from His seat at the centre, as the 'prime mover' of the solar system.) But conversely ideas themselves are experienced with almost physical ardour. Donne, who loved women with his wits, loved God with his senses.

'Intellectual' in this century has become a term in economics. 'Workers, peasants, and intellectuals', as the Russians say. To be an intellectual is not, necessarily, to be intelligent, or to be well informed. It may even be a sort of disease—ideas, like germs, being infectious—to be incapable of experiencing anything without the excitement of the mind, and usually the verbal part of the mind, playing a part in it. In love or death, in war or prayer, the intellect plays its part. And with the intellect, always, comes scepticism.

Those who saw the turn of the sixteenth century saw the passing of the Renaissance into the first dawning of the centuries of the Common Man, in the beginnings of Puritanism; they saw the last, superb expression of the ancient faith in Spanish Baroque art, and the Spanish Baroque saints; the highest point ever attained in Christian mysticism, in the period of Saint Teresa of Avila and Saint John of the Cross (both also poets) came late in the sixteenth century. Saint Teresa died in 1582, St John in 1591. But Copernicus had already set the round earth in motion, and the little world of his new astronomy was already a diminished part in an expanding universe, and Europe itself a diminishing part of a world in which America was already appearing on the western horizon. The medieval world and the modern, the setting and the rising stars, were in the sky together, for those who would to compare the values that had shaped the human world of the past, with those that were to shape its future. We ourselves, in a similar sadly privileged position, are well fitted to understand the basis from which arose Baroque art.

As the rift between the spiritual and the material values widened, the Great picked sides. England was then the great protagonist of the modern, Spain of the ancient, order. And in this polarity, English thought and poetry were strongly influenced by Spanish for the first and last time in history. The metaphysical poets are the fruits of this close contact with Spain, and that at a time when both countries were in their golden age.

In Spain, the great souls, confronted with the widening rift between material and spiritual orders, still chose the spiritual measure of life, even if it meant rejecting the earth, and all material things, since these seemed worthless, save in the context of the spiritual order of medieval Christianity. This is the meaning of the impulse, hard for the average human being of the twentieth century to understand, that sent young women of good family, with worldly prospects bright before them, into the reformed Carmelite houses that Saint Teresa had founded up and down Spain until her death in 1582.[1] Great and courageous souls like Saint Teresa herself and Saint John of the Cross, ascended so high above the conflict of faith and science that its divisions no longer reached them. And here be

---

1. To another century the irrational and often self-destructive desire to be a 'creative artist', so common at present among young people of both sexes, and so far from normal, will probably seem just as incomprehensible as the sixteenth-century urge towards the life of contemplative mysticism.

it said, that their mysticism was of a profundity and sophistication that a psychologist of Jung's stature may have standards to measure it, but not to invalidate it. If mental experience has a validity of its own, is entitled to be judged by its own standards, theirs was valid. But it rested on a foundation of rejection of the world. 'I die', Saint Teresa wrote, 'because I may not die'—for material life hung like an illusion between the soul and God. The earthly life she compared to a 'night in a bad inn'—and Saint John of the Cross, greater poet than she, was even more absolute in his rejection. With little more certainty of ever reaching another shore than the navigators who sailed across the Atlantic, they set out into 'the dark night of the soul' on a voyage of interior discovery no less courageous and hazardous, and in terms of human experience, no less richly repaid, than the contemporary explorers of the material world. Modern psychologists are content to analyse those visions of the mind without exploring them. These Saints, not content to observe, lived their discoveries of the heights and depths of interior experience.

In England, things went the other way. It was the world of the spirit, the 'interior castle' that was left to decay, while the discoveries of scientific materialism were pursued—to no less good purpose than were the spiritual by the Spanish religious minds. The strain characteristic of all Baroque art was felt on both sides. In Spain, Góngora and Gratian; in England John Donne and his school, bear the mark of the same attempt to hold together, in poetry, the two worlds; faith and material science; the finite and the infinite. In England, the spiritual was not quite forgotten; nor was the Spain of the counter-reformation able altogether to disregard the implications of the new material sciences. There was no longer one kind of truth in the world, but two, and those, so then it seemed, in conflict.

What was great in the Baroque poets was that they did not underrate either kind of truth. They tried to hold the two hemispheres (the very word is characteristic of Baroque poetry) together, and if even partially they succeeded, their achievement was a tremendous one. Then, as now, the price of seeing too clearly both systems of value, was conflict and unhappiness. But then, as now, neither the revolutionary nor the reactionary, both of whom see things more simply, was wholly civilized.

The greatness of Baroque art, therefore, may be seen to be not in its destructive element, but in its attempt to reconcile those kinds of knowledge that at certain times seem impossible to reconcile, except in art.

Professor Edouardo Sarmiento, writing of Spanish Baroque art,[2] points out how, the counter-reformation notwithstanding, even in Catholic Spain, this sense of strain reveals a latent doubt, disbelief, and loss of faith. 'If we may believe', he writes, 'the involuntary evidence of the art-style of an age for the state of its soul, then we cannot doubt that some such diagnosis of the Spanish counter-reform is true. The Baroque bears the stigmata of disbelief, anxiety, and decadence, as certainly as the Gothic bears the marks of faith, joy, and vigour.'

The strain characteristic of Baroque art is typically expressed in the use of perspective. In Baroque painting, the human figure is by this means seen to stand not firmly anchored to the earth, but is represented in often tormented and sensational attitudes rising towards heaven, or some other infinite point introduced into the composition by this exaggeration of perspective. In architecture, the typical façade is 'builded with the sky', to quote Professor Sarmiento again.

The extreme instance of an attempt to focus the finite on

2. *Bulletin of Spanish Studies*, July 1934.

the infinite, is to be found in the *transparente*—a kind of altar-piece found in some Spanish Baroque churches. Of this, Professor Sarmiento writes, 'When the central niche of the façade—a constructed altar grouping, is the throne for exposing the Sacred Host, the attempt to enclose the vista reaches its culmination. The serried mass of sculpture surges not merely round an outlet upon the heavens, but the Creator and Sustainer of the Heavens Himself, unmeasured contained physically within a white transparent circle of bread. Baroque paradox could go no further.'

But, he writes, 'Aesthetic order in a work of Art, which contains its own centre of reference, is the negation of the Classical, whose centre is one with the centre of life itself whether it is taken to be the earth, or the sun, or the other stars. And, even though unconsciously, its human orthodoxy is in danger—nay, has failed already.'

This may seem to be a digression from the subject—the meta-physical poetry of John Donne. But it is not so. For in poetry, a comparable attempt to bring together into focus the finite and the infinite, is the typical metaphysical figure, common to English and Spanish baroque poets, the conceit. Like the Baroque façade, this is not, as it might appear, a merely deco-rative device, but an attempt, in poetry, to harness together the tremendous forces of the temporal and the eternal, felt, as they were at that time, to be pulling apart. Here is a piece of John Donne from the poem 'Goodfriday 1613—Riding West-ward', in which the space—the literal physical poles of the earth—are straining against the Christian image.

> Let mans Soule be a Spheare, and then, in this,
> The intelligence that moves, devotion is,
> And as the other Spheares, by being growne

Subject to forraigne motions, lose their owne,
And being by others hurried every day,
Scarce in a yeare their naturall forme obey:
Pleasure or businesse, so, our Soules admit
For their first mover, and are whirld by it.
Hence is't, that I am carryed towards the West
This day, when my Soules forme bends towards the East.
There I should see a Sunne; by rising set,
And by that setting endlesse day beget;
But that Christ on this Crosse, did rise and fall,
Sinne had eternally benighted all.

In this poem, Donne achieves something, in poetic terms very like the *transparente* of Spanish Baroque architecture. The static image of Christ, the earth's fixed centre, is harnessed to the whirling image of the Copernican movement of the revolving earth, the moving spheres.

Could I behold those hands which span the Poles,
And turne all spheares at once, peirc'd with those holes?
Could I behold that endlesse height which is
Zenith to us, and our Antipodes,
Humbled below us? or that blood which is
The seat of all our Soules, if not of his,
Made durt of dust, or that flesh which was worne
By God, for his apparell, rag'd, and torne?

The tension is immense. But the poem holds as it intends to hold, the two orders of reality together, not scientifically, or theologically, but as poetry—the only force perhaps that can harness together truths of different orders.

That is an extreme example of the constant characteristic of the conceit, which is to bring together, using as a focal point some slight similarity between them, sharply contrasting images, belonging, often, to different orders of reality (as in the passage just quoted). Other figures are commonly used to accomplish the same end. Of metaphysical poems it is less the figures used than the purpose they serve that is characteristic. In this other quoted passage from 'The Relique', it is not science and the image of Christ that pull apart and are held by the conceit, but that other basic conflict that tormented the Baroque period, the paradox of life and death, sex and corruption.

> When my grave is broke up againe
> Some second ghest to entertaine,
> (For graves have learn'd that woman-head
> To be to more then one a Bed)
> And he that digs it, spies
> A bracelet of bright haire about the bone,
> Will he not let'us alone,
> And thinke that there a loving couple lies,
> Who thought that this device might be some way
> To make their soules, at the last busie day,
> Meet at this grave, and make a little stay?

There are other subsidiary antitheses; there is the juxtaposition of the old half-legendary medievalism, Adam and Eve in the Garden of Eden, Noah and the flood and the rest—with the new Copernican pattern of the world, as here:

> That unripe side of earth, that heavy clime
> That gives us man up now like *Adam's* time
> Before he ate; mans shape, that would yet be
> (Knew they not it, and fear'd beasts companie)
> So naked at this day, as though man there
> From Paradise so great a distance were,
> As yet the newes could not arrived bee
> Of *Adam's* tasting the forbidden tree.

Or again, the microcosm and the macrocosm are harnessed together in an image that recurs often in Donne, of life as land, death as sea:

> Man is the World, and death th'Ocean
>> To which God gives the lower parts of man.
> This sea invirons all, land though as yet
>> God hath set markes and bounds, twixt us and it,
> Yet doth it rore, and gnaw, and still pretend,
>> And breaks our bankes when ere it takes a friend.
> Then our land waters (teares of passion) vent;
>> Our waters, then, above the firmament,
> (Tears which our Soule doth for her sins let fall)
>> Take all a brakish tast, and funerall.

'My America, my newfound land,' Donne called his mistress. One meets everywhere images of latitude and longitude, lengthening and shortening shadows: the new Copernican framework of the universe. Superimposed on the human measure of the Christian myth with eternity and infinity, God-in-man, at the centre, is a new order in which eternity and infinity are being banished to the circumference of an expanding universe, no longer infinitely present, but infinitely remote.

John Donne was so placed in history, and so shaped by his personal experience, as to feel the pull of all those great forces that were rending the world apart at the end of the sixteenth century. His parents were Catholics; he had not only two Jesuit uncles (bringing him closely under the Spanish influence) but a martyr in the family three generations back—none less than Sir Thomas More, beheaded, for his allegiance to the Catholic faith in 1536. Through his stepfather, a distinguished London physician, John Symmings, twice president of the Royal College of Physicians, Donne made an early acquaintance with the paraphernalia of early natural science—and the terminology of human anatomy and physiology, bones, the functioning of the heart, lungs and nerves, forms yet another order of which Donne's poetry takes account.

His early tutors were Jesuits. From them he learned medieval philosophy, and the rules of the game of dialectics, that he played, cynically enough, in later life, when he was literary—or theological—ghost to the Revd Thomas Moreton, in controversies against his old friends the Jesuits in the terms he had learned from them. Like a later product of Jesuit education, James Joyce, Donne learned the game, but not a respect for the players. A glance at *Ignatius his Conclave*, proves both these points. In many other ways, too, Donne resembles Joyce. Both retained the Catholic foundations and scaffolding, on which both built monuments of scepticism. Both enjoyed playing with ideas and words like jugglers—more super-subtle than their Jesuit schoolmasters themselves. Both would have owed more to their teachers had they been loved a little more and taught a little less.

At fourteen, John Donne and his younger brother Henry went up to Oxford. Three years later, they went on to Trinity College, Cambridge, where, one imagines, the more speculative and modern atmosphere that there surrounded him, did something to untie the knots of Donne's early, and evidently unhappy, boyhood, and develop in him that spell-binding charm that by all accounts was his all his life. 'A kind of elegant, irresistible art,' Ben Jonson called it; and Izaak Walton describes his company as 'one of the delights of mankind'. Even now, in his rapid idiom, as close to the ordinary speech of his day as W. H. Auden's is to our own, one can almost catch the sound of his voice, even in the first poems:

> I Wonder by my troth, what thou, and I
> Did, till we lov'd? were we not wean'd till then?
> But suck'd on countrey pleasures, childishly?
> Or snorted we in the seaven sleepers den?
> T'was so; . . .

Want of beauty is a charge that has often been made against Donne's poetry; and in a certain sense with justice. For the worlds of beauty and of reality, too, were pulling apart at the turn of the century. Shakespeare wrote in a language at once near the real speech of men, and equally capable of speaking for that inner voice of the soul (heard all too often in the nineteenth century), for the two were not very different in an age when soldiers like Sidney and Essex, and seamen like Sir Walter Raleigh found it natural to be poets. But at the turn of the century, Shakespeare himself wrote:

> Truth may see, but cannot be,
> Beauty brag, but 'tis not she,
> Truth and beauty buried be.

Donne spoke a language stripped of magic, bare, in that sense, of beauty. Milton inherited the beauty, but no longer wrote poetry in a language that men spoke. One might see in this division, too, another symptom of the repression of the soul.

Two other experiences belonging to John Donne's youth gave colour to his picture of the world. The first was the death of his brother, Henry Donne who, at the age of twenty or twenty-one, died for his faith. Henry Donne, at a time when John was going to plays, making love to those sophisticated and painted women whom he so much liked, remained a fervent Catholic. He did what so many Catholics then were doing—sheltered a priest in his rooms at Lincoln's Inn. For this he was thrown into the Clink prison at Newgate, where he died of gaol fever.[3]

What Donne thought about this we do not know. Did he feel himself challenged to follow the family tradition of martyrdom that had claimed his grandfathers, his two uncles, and now his own brother? Was his anger directed mainly against those laws that made English Catholics outlaws in their own country? Or against that underground, narrow, jesuitical Catholic-minority background that had forced martyrdom on his brother? Was the Catholic religion worth such a price? Evidently he decided that it was not, for Donne never turned back to that early faith. Rather he threw himself into a life of pleasure and study, in the gay world of Elizabeth's London. But that Catholic shadow was always between him and Gloriana's worldly sun.

One other experience and Donne at twenty-seven must have felt himself able to say 'nihil humanum a me alienum puto'. In 1596, Donne joined Essex's expedition to raid Cadiz—the fashionable Spanish war of that year. There he saw war and yet another kind of death, in a burning Spanish ship—hideously modern.

> Out of a fired ship, which, by no way
> But drowning, could be rescued from the flame,
> Some men leap'd forth, and ever as they came
> Neere the foes ships, did by their shot decay;
> So all were lost, which in the ship were found,
>   They in the sea being burnt, they in the burnt ship
>   drown'd.

3. For this and other facts of Donne's life I am indebted to Miss Evelyn Hardy's book, *Donne: a Spirit in Conflict*, London (1942).

The following year he sailed, again under Essex, to the Azores. 'The Storme' and 'The Calme' show the poet knowing now the two horrors of life at sea—danger of death by shipwreck, and the stench and sickness of a ship becalmed in the tropics.

At the age of twenty-seven, Donne turned his mind to settling down. He became secretary to Sir Thomas Egerton, Lord Keeper of the Seal, father of two young men who had sailed with Donne under Essex. He was now an inmate of one of the greatest houses in London—York House, and a valued 'ornament' of that household. This must have seemed like the road to success. In this house Donne was near indeed to all the greatness of the court. But it was not Elizabeth's rising sun, but her decline that John Donne, the young secretary, saw in those four years at York House. His old leader the Earl of Essex, too, came to live under Sir Thomas Egerton's roof— but as a prisoner, under the Queen's displeasure. Here the Queen herself came as a visitor—but soon it was an old, broken woman who came to visit the young Earl, himself confined to his bed with sickness and sorrow. In 1600, Essex was beheaded. Whether or not John Donne saw with his own eyes that terrible execution, at which two or three blows were struck before the neck was severed, it must have stamped on his mind yet another of those images of death that seemed to lurk for him at the end of every avenue by which he sought to reach the secure sunshine of the world.

> sometimes in a beheaded man,
> Though at those two Red seas, which freely ranne,
> One from the Trunke, another from the Head,
> His soule be sail'd, to her eternall bed,
> His eyes will twinckle, and his tongue will roll,
> As though he beckned, and cal'd backe his soule.

At the turn of the century, it was not only Shakespeare who knew that

> Death is now the Phoenix' nest
> And the turtle's royal breast
> To eternity doth rest.

So, at the end of Elizabeth's reign, Donne had all the pieces in his hands. Scholasticism, science, adventure, war, both universities; London seen as a young man about town; and as a member of a household close to the court; vice he knew, and martyrdom. To call the fine suspense in which his mind hung in such a world cynicism would be to fail to understand the very essence of the civilized man's predicament. To be a cynic is to undervalue. Donne's strength was that he undervalued nothing. Each poem that he wrote is like a finely poised needle, suspended between the great magnets of science and religion, action and learning, the pleasures of love, the call to martyrdom; the infirm glory of the greatest court on earth; and the annihilation of all in death. The needle, for Donne, comes to rest only when it points to the one true North—that of love. And for Donne, as for Dante, it was through woman's love that his way lay towards the divine love that was his final point of rest.

In two of his longer works, we can see Donne's speculative mind at work in a way essentially modern, on changes of the medieval pattern of thought. 'The Progresse of the Soule', written in 1601, and one of Donne's finest poems, combines the Garden of Eden myth with a fine intuitive forecasting of modern biological theory. The transmigration of a 'soul', beginning its life in an apple on the tree of Eden, and ending just as it reached the human level (rather in mid-air, as Donne did not finish the poem as he had originally planned it) are traced from plant to bird, to fish, whale, elephant, dog, ape, and finally to man. Donne having no theory of science to prove cannot be blamed if the order is a little out at one or two places. But that the 'progresse' in the poem is so close to the picture that Darwin later established is a measure of the natural scientific bent of Donne's mind. And all this is combined in a series of Dürer-like pictures of plant and animal life, suggesting the herbals and bestiaries of the middle ages; in which walks Eve herself, as true to life as detail can make her; her mythical figure pulls up a real mandrake plant to give, as medicine, to a real baby. Like Dürer, Donne makes the myth credible by the realism of the detail.

Nine years later, in 1610, Donne wrote *Ignatius his Conclave*. This satire is amusing reading even now; Donne describes his 'vision', in which

> I had liberty to wander through all places, and to survey and reckon all the roomes, and all the volumes of the heavens, and to comprehend the situation, the dimensions, the nature, the people, and the policy, both of the swimming Illands, the *Planets* and of all those which are fixed in the firmament. Of which, I thinke it an honester part as yet to be silent, than to do *Galileo* wrong by speaking of it, who of late hath summoned the other worlds, the Stars to come nearer to him, and give him an account of themselves. Or to *Keppler*, who (as himselfe testifies of himselfe) *ever since* Tycho Braches *death hath received it into his care, that no new thing should be done in heaven without his knowledge.*

'In the twinckling of an eye', writes Donne,

> I saw all the roomes in Hell open to my sight. And by the benefit of certaine spectacles . . . (I know not of what making, but, I thinke, of the same, by which *Gregory*, the great,

and *Beda* did discerne so distinctly the soules of their friends;
when they were discharged from their bodies, and sometimes the soules of such men as they knew not by sight, and
of some that were never in the world, and yet they could
distinguish them flying into Heaven, or conversing with living men) I saw all the channels in the bowels of the Earth;
and all the inhabitants of all nations, and of all ages were
suddenly made familiar to me. I think truely, *Robert Aquinas*
when he tooke *Christs* long Oration, as he hung upon the
Crosse, did use some such instrument as this, but applied
to the eare; And so I thinke did he, which dedicated to
Adrian 6, the Sermon which *Christ* made in prayse of his
father *Joseph*; for else how did they heare that, which none
but they ever heard?

To proceed, Donne describes how (in Hell that is)

I saw a secret place, where there were not many, beside
Lucifer himselfe; to which, onely they had title, which had
so attempted any innovation in this life, that they gave an
affront to all antiquitie, and induced doubts, and anxieties,
and scruples, and after, a libertie of beleeving what they
would; at length established opinions, directly contrary to
all established before.

Here we recognize, in comic dress, the same Baroque conflict of ideas, of new and uncontrollable ideas that are far-
reaching enough quite to overturn the foundations of the
world. There is very little comic Baroque art, but *Ignatius his
Conclave* may be claimed as a rare example of this category.

In this imaginary 'hell' the Jesuits take a high place as the
arch equivocators. Here Donne 'saw' St Ignatius (like Jouvet,
in monk's habit) standing very close to Lucifer himself, advis-
ing him on the cases of those pretenders who sought admis-
sion to Hell's most exalted rank, as distorters of the universe.

The pretenders and their claims are interesting. Copernicus puts his case: 'Shall these gates be open to such as have innovated in small matters? and shall they be shut against me, who have turned the whole frame of the world, and am thereby almost a new "Creator"?' Ignatius opposes his claim. 'What cares hee', Ignatius asks, 'whether the earth travell, or stand still? Hath your raising up of the earth into heaven, brought men to that confidence, that they build new towers or threaten God againe? Or do they out of this motion of the earth conclude, that there is no hell, or deny the punishment of sin? Do not men beleeve? do they not live just, as they did before?' Also 'those opinions of yours may very well be true'—and that in itself must exclude Copernicus from the highest honours of Hell. In the light of subsequent history, one is inclined to think that Donne's Ignatius was premature in his conclusion that men went on living 'just as they did before' after Copernicus.

Paracelsus was excluded likewise, because such as his discoveries were, they were of minor importance. Machiavelli had a better case:

'although the entrance into this place may be decreed to none, but the Innovators, and onely such of them as have dealt in *Christian* businesse; and of them also, to those only which have had the fortune to doe much harme, I cannot see but that next to the Jesuites, I must bee invited to enter, since I did not onely teach those wayes, by which, thorough *perfidiousness* and *dissembling of Religion*, a man might possesse, and usurpe upon the liberty of free *Commonwealths*; but also did arme and furnish the people with my instructions, how when they were under this oppression, they might safeliest conspire, and remove a *tyrant*, or revenge themselves of their *Prince*, and redeeme their former losses; so that from both sides, both from *Prince* and *People*, I brought an aboundant harvest, and a noble encrease to this kingdome.' By this time I perceived *Lucifer* to bee much moved with this Oration, and to incline much towards *Machiavel*. For he did acknowledge him to bee a kind of *Patriarke*, of those whom they call *Laymen*. And he had long observed, that the *Clergie* of *Rome* tumbled downe to *Hell* daily, easily, voluntarily, and by troupes, because they were accustomed to sinne against their conscience, and knowledge; but that the *Layitie* sinning out of a slouthfulnesse, and negligence of finding the truth, did rather offend by ignorance, and omission. And therefore he thought himselfe bound to reward *Machiavel*, which had awakened this drowsie and implicite *Layitie* to greater, and more bloody undertakings.

'Vision' or not, what Donne wrote had this much truth in it. These were ideas whose conflict was on an earthly plan 'inducing doubts, and anxieties, and scruples, and after, a liberty of believing what they would'.

Between the Horatian vein of Donne's early love poems, and 'The Ecstasie', written in the early days of his love for his wife (then still Anne More, niece of Sir Thomas Egerton, queening it, at seventeen, as hostess for her widowed uncle at York House) is a difference not of degree but of kind. No poet has ever written more convincingly against fidelity in love:

> Will no other vice content you?
> Wil it not serve your turn to do, as did your mothers?
> Or have you all old vices spent, and now would find
>   out others?
> Or doth a feare that men are true, torment you?
> Oh we are not – be not you so
> Let mee, and doe you, twenty know.
> Rob mee, but binde me not, and let me goe.

Must I, who came to travaile thorow you,
Grow your fixt subject, because you are true?

Now he was to find that love is a stronger power than pleasure,

As our blood labours to beget
Spirits, as like soules as it can,
Because such fingers need to knit
The subtile knot, that makes us man.

And after a year of that marital love, he could write, and truthfully,

All other things, to their destruction draw,
Only our love hath no decay;
This, no tomorrow hath, nor yesterday,
Running it never runs from us away,
But truly keepes his first, last, everlasting day.

This was the marriage that has been written off by nearly all his biographers as the most unfortunate thing Donne ever did, and so it was. But, as is so often the case with our worst mistakes, it was also the best thing he had done so far. It was both these. And while it ruined his career for many years to come—for the scandal of Donne's runaway match with Anne More lost him his position in the York House, and effectively barred to him any other preferment—it is no less certain that, with his marriage, Donne's writings take on a mature nobility, a depth of understanding, from this time, that was to mature with the years. A love begun so unwisely in a setting so romantic, survived years of shared poverty, hardship, loneliness, and social banishment; a growing family, the sickness and loss of children. It was, in fact, a real marriage, from which Donne was to learn not only the joyful, but also the sorrowful mysteries of love.

During the fifteen years following his marriage, the current of love flowed underground, worked in secret. Outwardly, we see Donne frustrated with no outlet for his great mental energies, no scope for his remarkable abilities, living poorly in the country, which he always hated; then in a small unhealthy house at Mitcham; then under the roof of a patron, Sir Robert Drury. For a time he acted as literary ghost to his friend the Revd Thomas Moreton, afterwards Bishop of Durham. Donne, with his tongue in his cheek, must have enjoyed writing long controversial pieces against his old friends the Jesuits, employing against them the arguments they had taught him to use. The simpler mind of Thomas Moreton probably did not grasp the fact that Donne believed no more in his own arguments than in theirs; and it was he who first suggested to Donne that he should take Anglican orders—a suggestion that he made with admirable kindness and tact. But Donne refused on that occasion, giving as his reason, his own unworthiness for that profession.

Now when a man refuses the hand of an eligible young woman of good connections on the grounds of his own unworthiness, it may be, and very likely is, true that he is unworthy. But it is quite certain that he is not in love. Unworthiness is an unimpeachable excuse for getting out of the marriage without offending the family. Donne may have been unworthy to take holy orders. He was certainly not in love with the Anglican Church.

Donne's middle period—the years of poverty and worry that drove him to the necessity of a servility to possible patrons that became him very ill; in a series of always frustrated attempts to get back into a career of some sort—produced no poems as fine in their kind as the early *Songs and Sonnets*, or later *Holy Sonnets* and religious verse. But those he wrote at

that time are revealing, bringing to light as they do the measure of the spiritual maladjustment of Donne to his world, and
that world to itself; and the growing seriousness with which
the poet now sought to find a solution for a problem whose
implications he increasingly realized. The clue is to be found
in *The Anatomie of the World*, and the *First and Second Anni-
versaries*. These ambitious poems, full of fine passages, have
something deeply wrong about them, and are embarrassing
reading even now. This is not so much because they were written to some extent (possibly, or partly) with an eye to getting
a patron (which they did), but because they open a religious
void that it is saddening to contemplate.

These Rilke-like poems were written, like the *Duino Elegies*, on the occasion of the untimely death of a young girl—
a girl whom the poet had never seen—Miss Elizabeth Drury,
only daughter of that Sir Robert Drury who was to be Donne's
patron for a number of years. And if ever poems rang false,
these do. 'If It had been written of the Virgin Mary it had been
something,' Ben Jonson said of the *Anatomie of the World*—
and he has put his finger on the very point of the weakness.
They were not written of the Virgin Mary. They were, however (as Donne said), written 'of the idea of a woman, not
as she was'. They were, in fact, a lamentable, trumped-up
attempt to put a personal image and personal 'idea of a woman'
in the place of the old and universal Christian pantheon—even
of the Mother of God herself—who were gone from the
empty niches of the reformed churches of England. This
pompous, inflated, home-made improvisation tagged on to
the corpse of Miss Elizabeth Drury reveals just how far adu-
lation falls short of canonization. The root of medieval faith
had been severed. Not one of the elegies that Donne wrote in
succeeding years, attributing to the nobility and to princes
virtues that they may have possessed, or may not, ever could

bridge that gulf between the scepticism of the reform and the lost medieval faith. They remain mere epitaphs: these poems, and all Donne's poetry of the grave and the dead, is like a dark after-image of the light of faith and bears to the medieval faith the skull-like resemblance that the negative photograph bears to the positive.

Donne did indeed, like an apostle not of faith but of mortality, put something in those empty niches, in those churches deserted by their saints. But not the carved angels, not the shrines of gothic saints. He hung those empty walls with emblems of mortality, urns, marmoreals, symbols of death and physical corruption; the pomp of the grave, not the symbols of life. These silent testimonies of doubt have, in the English churches, replaced the saints in their shrines. Donne was, of that tradition, one of the originators, who left imprinted on the English Church its characteristic grand, but essential, though reluctant, scepticism. The real root of the reformation is for ever silently testified by these. The monument of Donne himself, in his marble winding-sheet, as it remains in St Paul's to this day, contrasts sombrely with the enshrined saints of the ages and places where death is not accompanied by the shudder of the grave, but by hope of heaven and fear of hell.

And yet there is greatness in the scepticism of the reform— for it is a relative, not an absolute scepticism that we find in the English Baroque; a scepticism that would fain believe, not one that belittles with the diabolical 'spirit that denies'. One that does still, in fact, hold to the desirability of faith, and therewith, some faith also. Like the Five Cups in the Tarot Pack, three are empty but two remain. The Anglicanism of Donne's day reflects like the moon, the last light from the setting sun of medieval Christianity. But the victory over 'superstitious practices' had been, by 1600, all too complete. The moon, too, was losing its reflected light, as that sun set on England.

A new tradition was to grow in the English Church. But the English Bible, its greatest ornament, was, in the reign of James I, still in translation. The magnificent words of the English Prayer Book were still unhallowed by time. And the emblems of mortality had not gathered dust. The grave yawned wide, and the stench and the worms of it became all man's future since what lay beyond it was less certain than it had been. In the Middle Ages, men had feared hell. Donne must have wished that the certain fear of hell would remove for him the greater horror of doubt, for if there is no hell, all must perish in the grave, in mortality, in annihilation.

Donne was still man enough of the Renaissance to feel that the death of one human being could matter. His pride and dignity were undulled by modern statistics into the accidia of a sense of anonymity, and the belief, that after all, it does not greatly matter that we die. Death mattered to Donne as much as heaven mattered to the saints. He gave to death, the adversary, his own stature, the greatness of a man of a court of the Renaissance.

If John Donne was resolved not to take Anglican orders, there was one person, and that a great one, resolved that he should—King James himself. The King who gave so many treasures to that Church—the final version of the Prayer Book, the English Bible—gave it also the Dean of St Paul's. For a long time the King had had an eye on Donne, and finally giving a point-blank refusal to all Donne's attempts to obtain preferment in other fields—as an ambassador, or in any other secular appointment, the King said in so many words, that he would give him advancement in the Church, but in no other profession. The old King, eccentric, lacking in charm and grandeur as he was, did well by the Church of England, and not least, when he gave it John Donne, who finally, in 1614, consented to be ordained.

It is true that this was not the career that Donne would have chosen. It is true that the Anglican Church would never be, for Donne, what the Catholic faith has ceased to be. Anglicanism was not an alternative faith, but a relative, though not absolute, scepticism; Donne himself was a relative—but not absolute— sceptic. But to imagine that Donne cynically entered the Church only because he could no longer endure to live without a position in the world and a source of income to support his family would be as wrong as to see Donne as a fervent Anglo-Catholic. Donne was far too spiritual a man to live without a religion. He was far too intelligent a man to be impressed either way by doctrinal controversy (had he not written it himself?). But God he conceived as far above such human conflicts, undignified, embittered and cruel as they were. In one of his early satires—on religious controversy—he had written, before 1597, on the quarrels that occupied the kings of England and of Spain, the Pope, Luther, and the rest,

> Foole and wretch, wilt thou let they Soule be tyed
> To mans lawes, by which she shall not be tryed
> At the last day? Oh, will it then boot thee
> To say a Philip, or a Gregory,
> A Harry or a Martin taught thee this?
> Is not this excuse for mere contraries,
> Equally strong? cannot both sides say so?
> That thou mayest rightly obey power, her bounds know;

—concluding—a conclusion that he maintained for the rest of his life—

> So perish Soules, which more chuse mens unjust
> Power from God claym'd, then God himselfe to trust.

The tide in England just then was carrying the more generous, living, vital things, in the direction of the reform. Donne was charitable, moderate and tolerant, and would rather compromise than prolong a bitter division. He could not fail to have been impressed by his good friends Bishop Moreton, Magdalen Herbert, the mother of George Herbert, the poet, and Lord Herbert of Cherbury; the Countess of Bedford, whose house at Twickenham had for Donne been like a garden of sweetness in his desert; and many others; all must have drawn Donne imperceptibly into a circle of friendship and understanding that, as the years passed, made the Church of England seem less alien to the son of an old Catholic family. So at last it came about that Donne had a secure place in the world. Soon he was to be that Dean of St Paul's, whom we remember as a kind of Anglican saint of mortality, an ornament of that cold, but not ignoble Baroque religion that has so well suited the English character, too speculative for absolute faith, but too idealistic for absolute scepticism. And as he lay dying, twenty years later, Donne could say truthfully, that he believed that the hand of God had been in the shaping of his life. It would be an impertinence to doubt that it was so.

Two years after Donne's ordination, and four before his appointment as Dean of St Paul's, Anne Donne died in giving birth to their twelfth child. If one sees the events of a life as stages of a pilgrimage, it is difficult not to see in Anne Donne's death the departure of one of those legendary guides—like Dante's Virgil, or Beatrice, who stayed with the poet only until her work was accomplished, for now Donne had entered the last stage of his strange development. Henceforth his inner life was to be lived in relation only to God.

Look at the beginning of Donne's life—those love poems, so subtly introspective, yet so worldly, so far from serious; at the portrait of Jack Donne at eighteen, the young man with the earrings, at the end of his three years at Cambridge; and look at the end—the eloquent divine, who, in the words of one critic, now 'put a trumpet to his lips'; who himself chose that posterity should remember him in the aspect of his death, the features burned out, the winding sheet tied about his face. How did the one change into the other? It happened imperceptibly, naturally. It is the same man. That unmistakable personal idiom, the rapid ardent sentences, the very imagery of the early love poems are found in the *Holy Sonnets*. The very imagery of erotic love is retained, and amplified into a symbolic language to speak of God, and to God.

> Take mee to you, imprison mee, for I
> Except you'enthrall mee, never shall be free,
> Nor ever chast, except you ravish mee.

The first and the last poems that he wrote, use almost precisely the same images.

Donne indeed put a trumpet to his lips in those later years, when he preached at Paul's Cross, to the people, and before two kings—James I, and later King Charles—at Whitehall; when he summoned up the angels in Baroque imagery of unsurpassed grandeur—

> At the round earth's imagin'd comers, blow
> Your trumpets, Angells, and arise, arise
> From death, you numberlesse infinities
> Of soules, and to your scattred bodies goe,
> All whom the flood did, and fire shall o'erthrow,
> All whom warre, dearth, age, agues, tyrannies,
> Despaire, law, chance, hath slaine, and you whose eyes,
> Shall behold God, and never tast deaths woe.

But a trumpet does not necessarily mean a release from doubts. With Donne, the light and shade was deeper, that was all, as his life declined from evening into night. In his youth, that we cannot know all seemed reason to doubt God; in his maturity, a reason for trusting Him. But as the noon of love darkened into the shadow of death, the witty scepticism of youth darkened into the agonizing doubts of age. It is still a poetry of doubt, of decline from faith, struggling to find certainty at the brink of the grave, that no other times of life, neither the love nor the learning of his prime, had yielded the poet. For all Donne's doubts gradually focused on one point— Death. As in loving women he was introspective, analysing his love, so in his sickness he analysed himself as thoroughly as Freud could ever have searched the submerged regions of instinct and the unconscious. If only he could have found the soul, and brought it out like an undiscovered organ! But deep as he might search, it was not to be found. The *Devotions on Sundrie Occasions* are in their way as searchingly introspective as the *Ascent of Mount Carmel*. But they are the voice of the body, the unconscious, the dark chaos of man, not his incandescence, as is St John's great introspective analysis.

To pass over the twenty years of his preaching and ministry, we reach the story of Donne's death. In the winter of 1630, Donne was a dying man. He was too ill to preach at Christmas, but at the beginning of Lent, knowing that it was for the last time, he rose from his bed to preach perhaps his greatest sermon of all—'Death's Duell, or A Consolation to the Soul against the Dying Life, and Living Death of the Body'. This sermon was 'Delivered at Whitehall, before the King's Majesty' on 25 February 1630, 'Being his last Sermon and called by His Majesties' Household, the Doctor's owne Funerall Sermon'. He took as his text the terrible sentence 'And unto God the Lord, belong the issues of death'. Here at its most sublime is that 'metaphysical shudder', the horror of mortality. Here indeed is Freud's death instinct, Rilke's little skull born with every living child, Hamlet's skull:

> Wee have a winding sheete in our Mother's wombe, which grows with us from our conception, and wee come into the world, wound up in that winding sheet, for wee come to seeke a grave; And as prisoners discharg'd of actions may lie for fees, so when the wombe hath discharg'd us, yet we are bound to it by cordes of flesh by such a string, as that wee cannot goe thence, nor stay there. Wee celebrate our owne funeralls with cries, even at our birth; as though our threescore and ten years of life were spent in our mother's labour, and our circle made up in the first point thereof. We begge one Baptisme with a Sacament of teares; And we come into a world that lasts many ages, but wee last not.

But in the very toils of this death, Donne was to portray, as it has never before or since been portrayed in England in poetry, or in any other art, the scene of the Crucufixion, in a baroque magnificence comparable only to the painting of El Greco:

> There now hangs that sacred Body upon the Crosse, rebaptized in his owne teares and sweat, and embalmed in his owne blood alive. There are those bowells of compassion, which are so conspicuous, so manifested, as that you may see them, through his wounds. There those glorious eyes grew faint in their light: so as the Sun ashamed to survive them, departed with his light too. And then that Sonne of God, who was never from us, and yet had now come a new way unto us in assuming our nature, delivers that soule (which was never out of his Father's hand) by a new way, a voluntary emission of it into his Father's hands; For though to this God our Lord, belong'd these issues of death, so that considered in his owne contract, he must necessarily die, yet at no breach or battery, which they had made upon his sacred Body issued his soule, but emisit, hee gave up the Ghost, and as God breathed a soule into the first Adam, so

this second Adam breathed his soule into God, into the hands of God.

There wee leave you in that blessed dependancy, to hang upon him that hangs upon the Crosse, there bath in his teares, there suck at his woundes, and lie downe in peace in his grave, till hee vouchsafe you a resurrection, and an ascension into that Kingdome; which he hath purchas'd for you, with the inestimable price of his incorruptible blood.

Here again we have doubt at its most heroic, redeemed by its own intensity, and achieving the stature of faith. For greater than a complacent belief in something trivial, is the doubt of something great. For to doubt is in itself to assert and establish the values doubted. So Baroque art takes its stature from medieval faith. Never again, perhaps, will a decline of faith produce anything comparable, for never again will the world have so much to lose, as the medieval Christian faith. Compared with the struggle with which then were relinquished the values of a passing age, it is frightening to see, in our period, with what ease, what lack of spiritual struggle, values are discarded. For the gulf that opens for us (in *Mein Kampf*, the Communist Manifesto, and our own and the American materialist Utopias) is as much deeper than Donne's relative doubt as medieval Christianity was higher than the liberal humanism that succeeded it, and is now in its turn the vanishing faith.

The image of Christ crucified is, of all the Christian images, the one that in itself contains the full paradox of human doubt and human faith, the focal point of temporal and eternal, at which the eternal is at once most essentially challenged, and most essentially triumphant. For Donne, the pull was not only away from faith, but also, with equal, and perhaps finally with greater strength, towards it. At the end of his life only two magnets retained any power over him—the image of the grave and the image of God.

In the seven weeks that lay between the preaching of 'Death's Duell' and death itself, Donne prepared for his promised end, still seeking God with a courage equal to that of any saint who ever battled his way out of this world. Yet it is as an emblem of mortality that Donne chose that we should remember him. Sir Izaak Walton tells how he

> sent for a carver to make for him in wood the figure of an urn, giving him directions for the compass and height of it; and to bring with it a board, of the just height of his body. These being got, then without delay a choice painter was got to be in readiness to draw his picture, which was taken as followeth: Several charcoal fires being first made in his large study, he brought with him into that place his winding-sheet in his hand, and having put on all his clothes, had this sheet put on him, and so tied with knots at his head and feet, and his hands so placed as dead bodies are usually fitted, to be shrouded or put into their coffin or grave. Upon this urn he thus stood, with his eyes shut, and with so much of the sheet turned aside as might show his lean, pale, and death-like face, which was purposely turned towards the east, from whence he expected the second coming of his and our Saviour Jesus. In this posture he was drawn at the just height; and when the picture was fully finished, he caused it to be set by his bed side, where it continued and became his hourly object till his death, and was then given to his dearest friend and executor, Dr. Henry King, then chief Residentiary of St Paul's, who caused him to be thus carved in one entire piece of white marble, as it now stands in that church.

To these last weeks also belong two of the greatest of his lyrical poems—the 'Hymn to God my God, in my sicknesse', and 'A Hymne to God the Father'.

In the first Donne, for a moment echoing the faith of Saint John of the Cross who wrote of the soul:

> Oh night that was my guide!
> Oh darkness dearer than the morning pride,
> Oh night that joined the lover
> To the beloved bridge
> Transfiguring them each into the other.[4]

writes like a mystic,

> Since I am coming to that Holy roome,
> Where, with thy Quire of Saints for evermore
> I shall be made thy Musique.

He takes his last backward look on the world. How long ago it was that he had written of his mistress' body, 'Without sharp North, without declining West'.

How long ago those voyages with Essex, long dead, to Cadiz and the Azores! Now these images of life are seen down the lengthening perspective of death:

> Whilst my Physitians by their love are growne
>   Cosmographers, and I their Mapp, who lie
> Flat on his bed, that by them may be showne
>   That this is my South-west discoverie
>   *Per fretum febris*, by these streights to die,
>
> I joy, that in these straits, I see my West;
>   For, though theire currants yeeld return to none,
> What shall my West hurt me? As West and East
>   In all flatt Maps (and I am one) are one,
>   So death doth touch the Resurrection.

4. [From 'Song of the soul in rapture' translated by Roy Campbell, Harvil Press, London, 1951.]

And for the last time for centuries to come, the natural and the spiritual orders are brought together in a Baroque image of unsurpassed power; for one last time the poles of the natural world, of the human measure and of supernatural truth, were one:

> We thinke that *Paradise* and *Calvarie*,
>   *Christs Crosse*, and *Adams* tree, stood in one place;
> Looke Lord, and finde both *Adams* met in me;
>   As the first *Adams* sweat surrounds my face,
>   May the last *Adams* blood my soule embrace.

But to his very death, doubt and faith struggled for the soul of John Donne. His last written words were these:

> I have a sinne of feare, that when I have spunne
>   My last thred, I shall perish on the shore;
> Sweare by thy selfe, that at my death thy sonne
>   Shall shine as he shines now, and heretofore;
>   And, having done that, Thou haste done,
>   I feare no more.

It has remained for a painter of our own tormented age, Stanley Spencer, to paint the scene that the monument he himself designed has for so long obscured, of *John Donne arriving at the Gates of Heaven*. For though much had perished in doubt, enough faith finally remained to bring within their reach that heroic soul who welded together in his poetry the hemispheres of broken truth.

ℭ Shelley as a Mythological Poet

The turn of the eighteenth century saw a flowering of the Imagination in English poetry as brief as it was marvellous. This flowering has left its heritage, unvalued by the materialist culture of the past two hundred years, but awaiting its rediscovery as (in Yeats's words) 'wisdom and poetry return', as he believed they must. This will come about as it is realized that not reason but Imagination is the supreme faculty, is, in Blake's words, 'the human existence itself'. Two centuries of materialism in the English-speaking West have brought us to a point at which, for a majority, 'the real world' is the solid measurable world of 'matter' which in its nature has no place for immeasurable realities of mind and Imagination. Coleridge called Imagination 'a repetition in the finite mind of the infinite I AM', the creative power by whose agency we build our world 'on earth as it is in heaven', in the likeness of our innate vision. Whereas for the Abrahamic religions man is a creature other than and external to 'God', for the Oriental religions as for the Platonic tradition—and especially for Plotinus and the Neoplatonists—there is a divine presence innate in man and in all creation. Our world is real because it is the creation of the human imagination. Shelley himself defines poetry as 'the expression of the imagination' and continues:

> It awakens and enlarges the mind itself by rendering it the receptacle of a thousand unapprehended combinations of thought. Poetry lifts the veil from the hidden beauty of the world, and makes familiar objects be as if they were not familiar. Poetry enlarges the circumference of the imagination by replenishing it with thoughts of ever new delight . . . .

Imagination is a mental world, a world of which 'nature' is a language rather than an object to be described by language; and Shelley's world is above all a world of thought. One can say that all civilizations before our own have been concerned with thought and its values: indeed is not mind the human kingdom itself? The great works of the world's wisdom have been concerned with meanings and values, not with measurement of a material order. But does it, one may ask, make any great difference, since we all see and experience the World, whether we hold it to be an object external to us or an experience of the Imagination?

There is one great and all-important difference: to the materialist the world is a lifeless object, to the man of imagination the world is a living being, 'full of gods'. For the materialist the question is 'what' is nature, 'what' are its rocks and stones and trees, earth, air, fire and water, whereas for Imagination the question might more properly be 'who'. Who is the West Wind, spirit of inspiration, who the skylark, the cloud, the moon, who the rivers and the trees? So it was for all the great romantic poets: Blake saw nature as 'One Continued Vision of Fancy or Imagination' where 'The morning stars sang together and all the Sons of God shouted for joy', as in the Book of Job. For Wordsworth there is 'a motion and a spirit' that 'moves through all things' and for Shelley all lives with the life of the mind. There are 'subtle and fair spirits' whose homes are the dim caves of human thought. The language of Imagination is symbolic, that is to say nature is a language in which ideas, moods, meanings, find their correspondence, while at the same time the forms of nature take on meanings. Henry Corbin, taking his thought from the Persian Sufi philosopher-poets, has introduced the term 'imaginal' to describe the world of Imagination, as distinct from the word 'imaginary' which in modern parlance means simply unreal, non-existent.

But although all thought is symbolic, not all symbolic thought is mythological. Thus Wordsworth sees nature as a great epiphany of the one 'motion and spirit' that is everywhere present. Conversely, mythological themes may be treated in an historical and biographical manner as fictions as Tennyson's Idylls of King Arthur and the Holy Grail are treated as literal fact. Delightful as these narratives may be they are not mythological in Tennyson's treatment of them, nor are they in T. H. White's *The Sword in the Stone*, though they again become so in David Jones's 'The Hunt' and 'The Sleeping Lord'. But Shelley's 'Subtle and fair spirits' which inhabit the human mind live and move and have their being in the world of the Imagination; and are, for Shelley, redemptive and inspiring:

> From unremembered ages we
> Gentle guides and guardians be
> Of Heaven-oppressed mortality;
> And we breathe, and sicken not,
> The atmosphere of human thought:
> Be it dim, and dank, and grey,
> Like a storm-extinguished day,
> Travelled o'er by dying gleams,
>   Be it bright as all between
> Cloudless skies and windless streams,
>   Silent, liquid, and serene;
> As the birds within the wind,
>   As the fish within the wave,
> As the thoughts of man's own mind
> Float thro' all above the grave;
> We make there our liquid lair
> Voyaging cloudlike and unpent
> Thro' the boundless elements.

In terms of materialist definitions, invisible spirits by whatever name simply do not exist—they are imaginary. But if Imagination is the 'boundless element' in which we and our world exist, this world is reality itself. It is not nature that includes mind, but mind which includes the vision of the universe we call 'nature'. To many this is simply unthinkable, but from the standpoint of every spiritually grounded civilization it is the world of materialism that is limiting, imprisoning and mutilating to the living spirit, preventing the caged bird from flying in its proper element. Blake's call throughout his prophetic poems is a summons to the English nation, under the domination of the materialist thought whose fruit was the Industrial Revolution, to 'awake' from the 'deadly sleep' into which England had fallen. To the materialist mentality imaginative awakening seems illusion and self-deception, and denial thus becomes the highest wisdom for those who

> Charge Visionaries with deceiving
> And call Men wise for not Believing.

Shelley's *Prometheus Unbound* is a celebration of the return to life and joy of a world freed from the fetters of denial by the affirmation of love. One might describe it as a poem of transfiguration through love—to use a word from Christian theology—for Shelley—as indeed for the Christian theologians—'transfiguration' reveals things as they really are, not less but more than they seem to the common daily mind, the world as it really and for ever is. As the spirits sing

> We come from the mind
> Of human kind
> Which was late so dusk, and obscene and blind,
> Now 'tis an ocean
> Of clear emotion
> A heaven of serene and mighty motion,

From that deep abyss
Of wonder and bliss,
Whose caverns are crystal palaces;
From those skiey towers
Where Thought's crowned powers
Sit watching your dance, ye happy Hours!
. . .
And, beyond our eyes
The human love lies
Which makes all it gazes on Paradise.

Yeats, for whom Shelley is the supreme poet, recalls that image, 'And Shelley had his towers, thought's crowned powers he called them once. What for the materialist is illusion, for the Imagination is reality itself. Thus all in Shelley's world lives with the life of the mind itself; of Imagination that creates it. Sky-lark and Cloud, Sensitive-Plant, the charmed boat of the Witch of Atlas, are all living with the one life of the universe.' Yeats in his essay 'The Philosophy of Shelley's Poetry' writes that he is 'certain that the imagination has some way of lighting on the truth that the reason has not, and that its commandments, delivered when the body is still and the reason silent, are the most binding we can ever know'. And he continues that he has re-read *Prometheus Unbound* 'and it seems to me to have an even more certain place than I had thought, among the sacred books of the world'. Yeats goes on to say that Shelley, in *A Defence of Poetry* 'will have it that the poet and the lawgiver hold their station by right of the same faculty, the one uttering in words, and the other in the forms of society, his vision of the divine order, the Intellectual Beauty' for (in Shelley's words) poetry is 'the creation of actions according to the unchangeable process of human nature as existing in the mind of the creator, which is itself the image of all other minds'. This image of the mind of the creator is

Imagination, which Shelley calls 'intellectual beauty'—as did Plato, who was himself Shelley's supreme teacher. Shelley has been called an 'atheist' and indeed he rejected the Judaeo-Christian God of the Ten Commandments as a tyrannous demiurge—as had Blake before him. But in the *Defence of Poetry* he speaks of 'the divine order' and of 'the mind of the creator', and in *Prometheus Unbound* makes the distinction very clear between the Creator and the moral tyrant. Asia, the bride of Prometheus, puts to Demogorgon the question:

> *Asia.* Who made the living world?
> *Demogorgon.* God.
> *Asia.* Who made all
> That it contains? Thought, passion, reason, will,
> Imagination?
> *Demogorgon.* God: Almighty God.
> *Asia.* Who made that sense which, when the winds
> of spring
> In rarest visitation, or the voice
> Of one beloved heard by youth alone,
> Fills the faint eyes with falling tears which dim
> The radiant looks of unbewailing flowers,
> And leaves this peopled earth a solitude
> When it returns no more?
> *Demogorgon.* Merciful God.
> *Asia.* And who made terror, madness, crime, remorse,
> Which from the links of the great chain of things,
> To every thought within the mind of man
> Sway and drag heavily, and each one reels
> Under the load towards the pit of death;
> Abandoned hope, and love that turns to hate;
> And self-contempt, bitterer to drink than blood;
> Pain, whose unheeded and familiar speech
> Is howling, and keen shrieks, day after day;

And Hell, or the sharp fear of Hell?
Demogorgon.   He reigns.
Asia. Utter his name: a world pining in pain
Asks but his name: curses shall drag him down
Demogorgon. He reigns.

There follows a praise of Prometheus, friend of man, and denunciation of his enemy, ending with the question:

   Asia.   Declare
Who is his master? Is he too a slave?
Demogorgon. All spirits are enslaved which serve things
   evil:
Thou knowest if Jupiter be such or no.
   Asia. Whom called'st thou God?
Demogorgon.   I spoke but as ye
   speak;
For love is the supreme of living things.
   Asia. Who is the master of the slave?
Demogorgon.   If the abysm
Could vomit forth its secrets. But a voice
Is wanting, the deep truth is imageless;
For what would it avail to bid thee gaze
On the revolving world? What to bid speak
Fate, Time, Occasion, Chance, and Change? To these
All things are subject but eternal Love.
   Asia. So much I asked before, and my heart gave
The response thou hast given; and of such truths
Each to itself must be the oracle.

For the eighteenth and much of the nineteenth century there was no recognized alternative to Christianity except scepticism. One can only describe the English at that time (and even now) as spiritually, metaphysically and imaginatively illiterate. There was, however, another current, of which the

Romantic poets are each in a different way a product: this was a revival of Platonism. At the turn of the century Thomas Taylor the Platonist—called 'the English Pagan' made the first complete translation of Plato's works into English, besides Aristotle, most of Plotinus, Proclus and the other Alexandrian Neoplatonists.

Shelley was himself a proficient Greek scholar but he cannot fail to have been aware of Taylor's challenge to Christianity in the name of the Platonic theology—for it was as a religious (or metaphysical) alternative to Christianity that Taylor saw the canon of the Platonic writings. Taylor's contribution to a revival of Platonism was deeply resented by the Academic establishment, but was seminal among those engaged in imaginative thought, and especially the poets. Coleridge absorbed his writings as a schoolboy; he was an early friend of Blake, gave a series of lectures on the Platonic theology at the house of Blake's friend Flaxman the sculptor, appears in one of the novels of Shelley's friend Thomas Love Peacock, and Mary Wollstonecraft, mother of Mary Shelley, was at one time his lodger. Shelley's rejection of Christianity was that of a deeply versed Platonist, not that of a sceptic. Like Taylor he had no respect for Christian theology, and saw (as did Blake also) the moral law-giver of the Bible as a tyrannous illusion. Shelley's vision was a larger, more philosophically subtle, more metaphysically traditional alternative to Christianity, but one not likely to be understood by his contemporaries, whether the Anglican clergy who held absolute control of the Universities, or the emerging figures of science and technology whose material success in promoting the Industrial Revolution was to prevail. Shelley was in reality more deeply committed to a vision of man as a spiritual being than the Deist clergy of his time and place. Not in the Christian doctrine of the resurrection of the body but in the traditional Platonic and Vedic doctrine of the immortality of the soul he certainly believed. Plato's affirmation 'for who knows whether to live be not to die, and to die to live?', repeated from one to another poet and philosopher of the Hellenic world, lies at the heart of *Adonais*, Shelley's great celebration of Keats. Heraclitus' teaching the 'mortals are immortals, and immortals, mortals' is not fancy (as it can only seem to the ignorant modern West) but is an integral part of the Platonic theology. The generating soul 'dies' from eternity into the time world, to resume its native immortality at death, and it is this doctrine, not some fancy of his own, that Shelley affirms in those burning lines familiar to us all:

> The One remains, the many change and pass;
> Heaven's light for ever shines, Earth's shadows fly;
> Life, like a dome of many-coloured glass,
> Stains the white radiance of Eternity,
> Until death tramples it to fragments. – Die
> If thou wouldst be with that which thou dost seek!
> Follow where all is fled; – Rome's azure sky,
> Flowers, ruins, statues, music, words are weak
> The glory they transfuse with fitting truth to speak.

The time-world—Plato's 'moving image of eternity'—is a pale and imperfect image of the eternal world it reflects. Furthermore (in common with Blake and perhaps with Wordsworth also) Shelley clearly held the belief, common to the Hellenic world, the Jewish mystical tradition and India to this day, in reincarnation. Lines which most of Shelley's readers can only take as poetic fancy, he certainly did not intend as such:

> Is it that in some brighter sphere
> We part with friends we meet with here?
> Or do we see the future pass

Across the Present's dusky glass?
Or what is it that that makes us seem
To patch up fragments of a dream,
Part of which comes true, and part
Beats and trembles in the heart?

For Shelley we are 'pilgrims of eternity'.

Symbolic images are not arbitrary signs—light and darkness, sun and moon, wind and cloud, mountain peaks and underground caverns, dove and swan and albatross—all these correspond in the nature of things to the meanings from time immemorial associated with them; as do some human creations, towers, palaces, or Shelley's magic boats on magic journeys. Myth carries symbolic discourse a stage further, it personifies, it enacts, and its actors are what Yeats calls the eternal 'moods', the 'gods' of all pantheons, who correspond, as it seems, to (in Shelley's words) 'the unchangeable process of human nature as existing in the mind of the creator'. All myths relate parts of what Edwin Muir called the 'fable' of which every individual human story is an approximation and partial enactment. What the fable is we do not know, only certain parts of it, Imagination is ever at work weaving and revealing. In that timeless world, as in the 'once upon a time' of fairy-tales, as in our dreams, the 'laws of nature' give place to the 'laws of the Imagination' where thoughts are causes and effects magical. The psychology of C. G. Jung has restored to us at least a clue to the nature of mental and mythological worlds in which our ancestors were at home. The bleak factuality of materialist scientific doctrine is once again called into question by the Imagination. In that dimension Shelley moved habitually and with ease. Mythological discourse, in Shelley, unites what is in its own right imagery of the natural world of perfect precision and beauty, with meanings on another level, that of the Imagination. 'Ode to the West Wind' is at once a

marvellous description of the wind and storm blowing over
Italian skies, the behaviour of clouds charged with electricity
about to discharge itself; and 'wind' as an age-old symbol of
inspiration. Shelley can never be faulted in those beautiful
'correspondences' he always finds for the language of the soul.
The lark is at once the bird and the soaring impulse of joy;
cloud and moon, all the scale of nature on which he played as
a musician upon a keyboard, form that texture of beauty by
which he knew so well how to transport us on to another
plane, seldom realized in daily life, yet never remote or inaccessible. In *Hellas*, Shelley takes the figure of Ahasuerus from
the medieval legend of the 'wandering Jew' who is the death-
less possessor of cosmic knowledge, the archetypal figure Jung
calls 'the wise old man' who in different guises is to be found
in all mythologies, and visits our dreams imparting wisdom
beyond the reach of individual experience and the daily mind.
　　How like a dream is this passage of myth:

> He who would question him
> Must sail alone at sunset, where the stream
> Of Ocean sleeps around those foamless isles,
> When the young moon is westering as now,
> And when the pines of that bee-pasturing isle,
> And evening airs wander upon the wave;
> Green Erebinthus, quench the fiery shadow
> Of the gilt prow within the sapphire water.
> Then must the lonely helmsman cry aloud
> Ahasuerus! and the caverns round
> Will answer Ahasuerus! If his prayer
> Be granted, a faint meteor will arise
> Lighting him over Marmora, and a wind
> Will rush out of the sighing pine-forest,
> And with the wind a storm of harmony
> Unutterably sweet . . . .

It is not hard to understand from such passages why, for Yeats, Shelley is the supreme poet, uniting in his symbolic virtuosity images of the visible world with resonances of meaning and beauty of the immeasurable worlds of Imagination. What, as natural description, could surpass the fiery shadow of a gilt prow in sapphire water? The 'faint meteor', the wind that will 'rush out of the pine forest' with 'a storm of harmony'? The sunset where

> the stream
> Of Ocean sleeps around those foamless isles
> When the young moon is westering as now.

With what virtuosity does the poet use these images as a language of 'correspondence'—as metaphors for soul's country. As in our dreams each image is charged with meaning and feeling. No detail is added which does not serve— again as in our dreams—to communicate realities of another order. The time is twilight, between the light of common day and the mystery of darkness, 'between the sleeping and the waking mind', as Yeats has described the place of imaginative inspiration. The summoner of a secret wisdom must go alone, for his is an inner journey none can share. The 'sea-cavern' doubtless signifies for Shelley the Homeric Cave of the Nymphs, sacred shrine where life itself issues from a source hidden in impenetrable darkness. That mysterious cave where Ahasuerus dwells is the place of the "demonesi', daimons, spirit-messengers between worlds, intelligences known in other traditions as 'angels'—and indeed Shelley does so name them in the 'Ode to the West Wind', the same who on Jacob's Ladder ascend and descend between heaven and earth, the higher and lower worlds. Ahasuerus, archetype of cosmic knowledge, is to be summoned from the inner realms of soul itself—as in *Prometheus Unbound* Demogorgon makes Asia understand, 'of such truths/Each to itself must be the oracle'. Ahasuerus advises the Sultan who has come to consult him to

> Commune with
> That portion of thyself which was ere thou!
> Didst start for this brief race whose crown is death.

None can approach that frontier without awe, without the sense of the numinous which can be experienced but not defined. The inspired voice speaks of a mystery which is in its nature beyond the comprehension of reason. This is the realm of mythology, at once strange and familiar. Our remote ancestors moved within that world with ease, their records are their myths. We ourselves experience that world in our dreams; indeed we should read symbolic poetry and myth as we would interpret dreams and read our dreams as if they were poetry. That world is no less native to us than is the world of common day, and it is the art of imaginative poetry to open to us its frontier. Shelley also understood that this imaginative dimension is in reality present as a dimension in every life, and it is for the poet to reveal its presence. In *Epipsychidion*, the great love poem addressed to Emilia Viviani, Shelley's passionate indignation at the thought of this beautiful young woman taking the veil arose from his vision of the sacredness of the erotic; he sees the divine beauty in the woman of flesh and blood, and in the particular woman the presence of the goddess:

> the brightness
> Of her divinest presence trembles through
> Her limbs as underneath a cloud of dew
> Embodied in the windless Heaven of June
> Amid the splendour-winged stars, the Moon
> Burns, inextinguishably beautiful:
> And from her lips, as from a hyacinth full

Of honey-dew a liquid murmur drops,
Killing the sense with passion; sweet as stops
Of planetary music, heard in trance.
In her mild lights the starry spirits dance,
The sun-beams of those wells which ever leap
Under the lightnings of the soul – too deep
For the brief fathom-line of thought and sense.
The glory of her being, issuing thence
Stains the dead blank, cold air with a warm shade
Of unentangled intermixture, made
By love.

Paradoxically poets are the 'legislators of the world' not because they attend to those outer events that are the concern of politicians and journalists, but because they perceive inner realities, these being the spiritual causes of natural effects. Blake's great mythological narratives are concerned with the inner condition of England's national life at the time of the French, American and Industrial Revolutions. As a mythologist concerned with the world of causes, no poet has effected more in the world of history than did Shelley. It was Shelley who formulated the principle of non-violence as a power more potent than arms, and it was Shelley's *The Mask of Anarchy* that inspired Gandhi, who carried Shelley's seemingly impracticable dream into effect in a way that has changed the conscience of the world. But greater still I believe is the importance of Shelley's proclamation of the sacred nature of erotic love. In the Christian tradition sexual love was the cause of the 'fall' of man. With Shelley on the contrary Eros is redemptive. Rousseau had, in his *Confessions*, first made his plea for 'free love', and Mary Wollstonecraft, follower of Rousseau, had in her tragic life put into practice Rousseau's revolutionary principle. Shelley's second wife, Mary, was the daughter of this first feminist and of Godwin, the political theorist, whom she married, to die giving birth to Shelley's Mary. Shelley's older contemporary, Blake, had known and much admired Mary Wollstonecraft, two of whose books he had illustrated, and Blake's poem, *Visions of the Daughters of Albion*, an eloquent plea for free love, is clearly inspired by Mary. It seems likely that Blake would have given a copy of this poem to Mary, who had inspired it, and if so Shelley could have seen it in Godwin's house. Christianity, which exalts virginity and motherhood in the Blessed Virgin Mary, never at any time allowed a place for the erotic. For the first time, with Shelley (and to a lesser degree with Keats, whom Shelley passionately admired) the erotic was to enter English poetry not as the cause of the Fall of man but as a sacred and numinous reality. In his choice of Prometheus as the friend of man, Shelley was to transform Aeschylus' drama on the theme of Prometheus into a celebration of the power of love. Prometheus, benefactor of mankind, because he stole fire from the gods and gave it to men, was punished by Zeus, chained to a rock in the Caucasus, where the eagle, bird of Zeus, tore his liver, a torment daily renewed. In the version of Aeschylus Prometheus was freed because he held the secret of a prophecy that Thetis, a daughter of Poseidon, would bear a son greater than his father. By revealing this secret to Zeus, Prometheus prevented his union with Thetis who was married to Peleus, a mortal, and fathered Achilles—but Shelley was unwilling to allow the great friend of man to surrender to his enemy 'the tyrant of mankind'—indeed he had at one time thought of Milton's Satan as the heroic rebel. He changed the story, introducing Demogorgon as the son of Zeus by Thetis, greater than his father who was to lead in a new age in which love would be the supreme power and rule the world. Shelley understood that the world of myth—of Imagination—is a living, self-creating world and to be bound by history is not in its nature. Thus, while Prometheus and Jupiter are taken from Aeschylus, Demogorgon and Asia are of Shelley's creation, in accordance with what he himself discerned of the inner changes taking place behind the history of his own age. Blake too had proclaimed a 'New Age', and Wordsworth saw in the French Revolution a dawn of freedom.

There is in Aeschylus' drama no feminine figure, except Io, turned by jealous Hera into a cow, who in her wanderings visits Prometheus. Perhaps Io is vestigially present in Shelley's *Prometheus Unbound* in the form of Ione, who with Asia and Panthea (which simply means all-goddess) are the 'daughters of Ocean'. In a note by Mrs Shelley Asia is said to represent Venus, or Nature: why then is she named Asia? Shelley sets the scene of Prometheus' torment in 'a Ravine of icy rocks in the Indian Caucasus'. Now the Caucasus range is not in India, as Shelley must have known. The location belongs not to the geography of the planet but to the geography of the Imagination: the region of Prometheus' redemption is located on the border of the India of the Imagination for symbolic reasons. His beloved, his *Shakti*, Shelley names 'Asia' as if to say that the Promethean Western mind needs for its completion the feminine soul of the Orient. Asia can only be, in this context, 'India'; for the scene of the reunion of the liberated Prometheus with Asia is in 'that far Indian vale', 'a lovely vale in the Indian Caucasus'. The temple of Prometheus was formerly built

> beyond the peak
> Of Bacchic Nysa, Maenad-haunted mountain
> And beyond Indus with its tribute rivers.

The mention here of Bacchus and his Maenads is, again, geography of the Imagination, for Dionysus was the god of

Inspiration, and the Maenads are invoked in the 'Ode to the West Wind' in this context. Doubtless it would be possible to find 'sources' for Shelley's 'lovely Indian vale' in travellers' tales of the forests of Kashmir, but no accuracy or inaccuracy of description is needed to account for the rich imaginative landscape of symbolic correspondence:

> a cave
> All overgrown with trailing odorous plants
> Which curtain out the day with leaves and flowers,
> And paved with veined emerald, and a fountain
> Leaps in the midst with an awakening sound.
> From its curved roof the mountain's frozen tears
> Like snow or silver, or long diamond spires,
> Hang downward raining forth a doubtful light;
> And there is heard the ever-moving air
> Whispering without from tree to tree, and birds,
> And bees; and all around are mossy seats,
> And the rough walls are clothed with long soft grass;
> A simple dwelling, that shall be our own.

Rama and Sita built their bower in those same woods where all lovers dwell in their paradisal dream. The Ramayana is full of lovely luxurious descriptions of incense-bearing trees and lotus lakes; for the poetry of erotic love demands and itself creates those forest glades of unspoiled nature where 'The Champak odours fall/Like sweet thoughts in a dream' (Where did Shelley come to know the scent of Champak?)

But Shelley would never have created a character so central to his greatest work from vague impressions of exotic beauty gathered from travellers' tales. What could Shelley have known of Indian poetry? Charles Wilkins, friend and colleague of Sir William Jones (and friend of Dr Johnson) had published the first translation of the *Bhagavad Gītā* into English in 1785.

Blake knew this work, and Shelley, with his interest in things Indian, would certainly have done so; but although this great poem is spoken by the Lord Krishna to his cousin Arjuna on the battlefield of Kurukshetra, there is no mention in it of erotic love.

There are two works which Shelley is likely to have known, both translated by Sir William Jones himself. One is Kalidasa's *Shakuntala*, the story of a half-divine daughter of an Apsara who was found in the forest and married by the king of Bharat; this work was popular and widely read. Goethe is said to have admired it. The other is the *Gita Govinda*, written in the twelfth century by Jayadeva, celebrating the loves of the Lord Krishna and Radha one of the Gopis of Brindavan. The worship of the god Krishna throughout India is associated with Radha, his beloved, with Krishna as the divine flute-player who enchants and seduces the milkmaids of Brindavan. Jones's translation appeared in the *Proceedings of the Calcutta Society* in 1792 and although there is no record of Shelley having read it, it seems very unlikely that he had not. Would not the poet, his mind engaged in the theme of the sacredness of erotic love, in naming his goddess-figure 'Asia', and situating her home in India, have had better evidence than vague exoticism for choosing India, the home of the great cult of sacred erotic love? The *Gita Govinda* is the source of the widespread Bhakti cult of India, of numberless paintings of the love of Radha and Krishna, of the famous Circle dance performed in Brindavan to this day, and the most widely performed theme of the Indian classical dance. The supreme love theme of India is the love between Krishna, the divine lover and Radha. The erotic images are understood on several levels as the mystical union of the soul with God, but also as a celebration of the sacred nature of sexual love itself. The Krishna of the *Bhagavad Gītā* may have existed as a king in Northern India, but Radha is an invention of poetry, yet has become a goddess, whose myth is danced, painted, enacted and celebrated throughout India, with temples dedicated to Radha and her divine lover. Indeed I found myself, not so many years ago, at the very heart of Radha's festival celebrated on the feast of Holi at Brindavan where the child Krishna grew up among the gopis.

There is of course much in common between the Platonic and the Vedic tradition; but there are passages whose cosmic sweep seems to take their inspiration from the song of the Lord Krishna, the *Bhagavad Gītā*. In *Hellas* these words of Ahasuarus:

> this Whole
> Of sun, and worlds, and men, and beasts, and flowers
> With all the silent or tempestuous workings
> By which they have been, are, or cease to be,
> Is but a vision – all that it inherits
> Are motes of a sick eye, bubbles and dreams;
> Thought is its cradle and its grave, nor less
> The future and the past are idle shadows
> Of thought's eternal flight – they have no being:
> Nought is but that which feels itself to be.

The Shakespearean reference notwithstanding ('all that it inherits') 'thought's eternal flight' seems closer to India than to Plato. Be that as it may India has always had a deep love for the poetry of Shelley, at least until secularization and Westernization of Indian education began to destroy their great traditional culture. Shelley has been the most loved of the English poets; India has for Shelley a greater sense of affinity than he has ever enjoyed in his own country save from those who, like Yeats, were themselves seekers for spiritual knowledge. Indian friends have quoted to me, as an example of Shelley's closeness to Indian symbolic thought the penultimate stanza from *Adonais*:

> That Light whose smile kindles the Universe,
> That Beauty in which all things work and move,
> That Benediction which the eclipsing Curse
> Of birth can quench not, that sustaining Love
> Which through the web of being blindly wove
> By man and beast and earth and air and sea,
> Burns bright or dim, as each are mirrors of
> The fire for which all thirst; now beams on me,
> Consuming the last clouds of cold mortality.

Blake in his old age wrote his own reflection on those who live on earth as if it were already that other timeless world of mind or spirit, which to Imagination is more real than the shadow world of 'cold mortality'; he was surely remembering, besides Thomas Paine, those young revolutionary idealists who used to meet weekly at Johnson's bookshop in St Paul's Churchyard, when they were all young, among them Godwin and Mary Wollstonecraft; and his words apply no less to Shelley, child of that revolution:

> Many persons, such as Paine & Voltaire, with some of the Ancient Greeks, say: 'we will not converse concerning Good & Evil; we will live in Paradise & Liberty'. You may do so in Spirit, but not in the Mortal Body, as you pretend, till after the Last Judgment; for in Paradise they have no Corporeal & Mortal Body.

Shelley affirmed the sacred nature of sexual love, and in his attempt to live by that vision bruised himself and has ever since been condemned by those who live in 'the real world'. But to Shelley the vision was more real than the world of 'cold mortality' that has judged him, and he believed that, some day, the world will live according to the truth of the Imagination, under the rule of love. In his great poem, which Yeats names among 'the sacred books of the world', he gave that vision its vesture of poetry, as a reality of the human spirit already realized.

9 Wordsworth: A Remembered Experience

I was born in 1908 and as I come to write of my childhood find myself thinking of Edwin Muir's line, 'My youth to myself grown fabulous', so different was that long-ago world from that of even country children today. Both my parents were born in 1880; my father a schoolmaster—the son of a coalminer, of the Industrial Revolution—and my mother the daughter of a Scots country schoolmaster who had moved across the Border and taught a school in the remote moors of Kielder. I remember my grandparents' house and its garden bright with flowers—now it is under the waters of Kielder reservoir, and the open heather moors dense plantations of conifers. My parents had met as students at the Armstrong College in Newcastle, my father having risen through the old apprenticeship of becoming a 'pupil teacher', then taking his B.A. degree, and his M.Litt., for which his thesis was on Wordsworth.

Thus in several ways I grew up in Wordsworth's world; but my parents experienced that world very differently. My mother had grown up in the wilds among places and people not unlike those Wordsworth had known in adjacent Cumberland and Westmorland and has made for ever a part of the landscape of the English imagination. All my father's school holidays were spent in Northumberland, and during the First World War I was sent to live with my mother's family in a place I already loved; and there between the ages of eight and ten I lived the life of a Wordsworthian country child. My schoolfellows were the children of farmers and shepherds living on the farms they had most likely inherited from generations bearing their names, and who would certainly have been at some time to Newcastle but never to London—indeed Edinburgh seemed nearer, culturally speaking, in our Presbyterian world.

My father had never been in this sense a country child and seemed always alien in that world which was to me 'the real world', permanent and secure. His Wordsworth, I now surmise, was the Wordsworth of left-wing political idealism, for I remember his often quoting those lines about the French Revolution,

> Bliss was it in that dawn to be alive,
> But to be young was very Heaven.

My father still lived in the light of that new dawn; and his belief in mankind's innate goodness, once freed from whoever the 'tyrants' may have been, was unshakeable. I have in my own lifetime seen revolutions come and go—in Spain, in Russia—and seen how one day's glorious freedom becomes the next day's tyranny, and I find it hard to imagine that Wordsworth's youthful political enthusiasms can carry conviction any longer. But to many like my father the political idealism of the early nineteenth century—shared by Blake and Shelley as well as by the young Wordsworth—was an inspiration from which no doubt many excellent political reforms followed. But I cannot help but feel that the 'politics of time' (to use a phrase of the Irish mystical poet Æ) is a secondary matter to 'the politics of eternity' which is the real concern of those unacknowledged legislators of the world, the poets.

My mother was indifferent to politics, and *The Rights of Man* and the rest, Rousseau's heady wine that had so intoxicated Wordsworth's generation—and which through his poetry continued to inspire young idealists still hoping for a better world as the outcome of glorious revolution—she never drank. But she never failed to notice the violet by a mossy stone, the primrose by a river's brim, the murmuring sound of a swift burn with its pools and waterfalls, inhabiting the world of nature's inviolate places with no less love than did Dorothy Wordsworth herself; and it was my mother's world, not my father's, that I inhabited, that seemed to me the 'real world', in which the slag heaps and the machinery that were part of my father's people's mining village in County Durham—and indeed the rough lives of the miners and their families in their mean homes—seemed an outrage against the integrity and beauty of the earth, against what ought to be. I could not understand why slag heaps should be, all that seemed an appalling mistake, an outrage against the beauty of nature. I participated in the lives of my country school-fellows, and that seemed the only natural way of life. The London suburb where my father taught the sons of city commuters who travelled to 'the city' in third-class carriages in the morning to return in the evening; and the defilement of industrial villages and towns seemed a tragic and inexplicable mistake. As did whatever is ugly or vulgar—nature is never without some beauty to which the soul can turn for solace; and country people might be poor and were certainly ignorant of many things that civilization has bequeathed, but were not vulgar.

In such beliefs Wordsworth's poetry, as I received it from both my parents, confirmed me; and if to his ideas I paid little heed, the people and places of the Lyrical Ballads and all those poems dealing with country life and ways and places corresponded so completely with the world as I knew it and loved it that the poetry seemed no less part of the natural order of things than did the hills and the clouds and the snow and the winds themselves. Like the young Wordsworth I roamed free in the rocky hills and open moors as he had done as a child. My young heart assented to his vision of 'nature' in its dignity and grandeur and in its lovely close-at-hand, the lesser celandine, the sparrow's nest, the owls at night; to the drama of weather, storm, snow-bound winter, in a world where men and women still lived and died in the farms and cottages where they had been born. Their culture did not come from newspapers and 'the media'; the men had their rural skills, the women baked their weekly batches of loaves and pasties, churning butter, embroidering, making their own clothes, skills surely more rewarding than the 'freedom' to leave home for the city, like Michael's son Luke, type of all those prodigals who never return. Because undistracted by world-news real events carried with us their full weight and significance—births and deaths and weddings, or some story of lives going wrong, people had their full stature and dignity, and we heard the words of the Bible read Sunday by Sunday in our dignified seventeenth-century Presbyterian kirk; stories of country people of other lands but whose 'seed-time and harvest, summer and winter, day and night' were like our own, as were the storms and the mountains that inspired awe and lifted our eyes to the hills whence came divine help, through those age-old natural correspondences to the soul's moods and intuitions.

Or can one say that world was already over when I knew it by reason of the very causes that had doomed it: the First World War, the Industrial Revolution, the population explosion that drove people to the towns and the exile of London suburbs, without memory, without beauty? And was it not already doomed when Wordsworth described what was already threatened, is not his own story that of the Prodigal who seeks to return only to find that we cannot re-enter the past? For all he returned to the loved places after his adventure in the worlds of London and of revolutionary France, these were no longer the places he remembered for he was no longer the child who was 'father to the man', who returned. Wordsworth's story tells of Paradise Lost unwillingly, a loss perhaps never to be fully accepted by the poet; who, for all he returned to his beloved Westmorland never again re-entered the living experience of 'nature' he had known. For he himself had undergone education at Cambridge, undergone history, undergone the first shocks of a revolution which was not to realize those high hopes of his for mankind, but rather to sweep away that rural culture which from time immemorial had been the norm of human life on earth: not for the Promised Land but for the exile of modern industrial cities. Already when he set out so joyfully for Cambridge he had left that primordial world and its timeless ways to become a stranger in a strange land, however seductive the pleasures of exile may at times have been. And for all the 'bliss' of the French Revolution, that revolution was the way of no return for Western civilization.

Yet what I would call the 'Wordsworth experience' has seemed to those of us who lived within it an affirmation of the timeless, the permanent, to be a celebration of the enduring grass roots of life, in harmony with the cosmos itself, whose children we are. But how many children now, even among those living not in cities but in what is still called I suppose 'the country' can experience that sense of nature's protective embrace and the wisdom of her teaching that Wordsworth celebrates? How much of his poetry is 'relevant' to times and places so different? Roads and railways, trains and motor cars and buses have penetrated the remote places, shrinking the scale of the great hills and empty spaces. So even more have telephones and radio and television brought the distant places within the same network of experience as our inner cities. The manse at Bavington where I lived in the far-off years had neither water-closet, taps nor electric light. Instead we had a well of spring water and a water barrel to collect the rain, candles and oil lamps and the *Northern Presbyter* once a week (or was it once a month?) by way of news of the outside world. Like Wordsworth and Dorothy, when we visited our friends on distant farms we walked. The local farmers and their wives drove to church on Sundays in traps; farmers and their sons rode on horseback and I seem to remember there were donkeys too. But the natural scale, so to say, of the world yielded rich joys, the plants and the birds of the roadsides were close to us, and the hills kept their dignity of distance, as we moved in, not through, our world. The weather made drama enough of these comings and goings. Lost lambs on ledges, a bull loose from the bull field, the fidelity of a sheepdog were realities of our lives, and all that happened within a community of neighbours who had known one another for better and worse for years had the significance of the Border Ballads whose descendants still bore proudly the old names. Now the television set brings into the remotest kitchens, be these in the Outer Hebrides, Indian villages in the Deccan or native American reservations in Southern Arizona, instantaneous news of the whole planet; every solitude has become permeable. In my own remote hamlet weekenders occupy the cottages abandoned by the country people, farmers' daughters spend their honeymoon in the Caribbean or on travelling round the world. The world Wordsworth describes has receded from those hills and valleys, dear to tourists, where speedboats tear the silence of Ullswater and Windermere and holiday caravans line their shores. Yet it is in search of lost paradise that tourists themselves come, and perhaps for a moment we may be blessed by the ever-presence of nature. And yet each modern improvement, each labour-saving invention of mass production, our souls experience as a loss, a deprivation, an alienation — such is the paradox. And what, I wonder as I re-read poems that once seemed to have grown out of the very world I inhabited, does the modern urban reader discover in those celebrations of a vanished world?

Much, I believe; for it is in my own lifetime that the motor car, the telephone and the television have transformed us from children of nature to children of the cities. And what are two or three generations to us, who from time immemorial have been children of the living earth, companioned by the hills and the stars, clouds, birds and animals, summer and winter, day and night? I believe we are still what heaven and earth have made us, the elements, and the ever-changing never-changing epiphany of nature that Wordsworth celebrated, even now more native and familiar to us than our technological environment can ever be. Do we not live in exile from our real selves, in a sort of second self, a self without memory, which we construct in order to survive in that exile? But that second nature which with such ease adapts to all those modern inventions with which we insulate ourselves, is only a superstructure. We discover in the abiding world of nature our older, truer selves. I do not believe that such as I, who remember that vanished world, are alone in the grass-roots rural world of people, and in the natural world Wordsworth experienced with so much love, and that his poetry has bequeathed us a human norm. In our marvellous cities we live as exiles. From Hesiod to Virgil to Robert Frost and Rabindranath Tagore men and women have lived in the embrace of nature since Adam delved and Eve span. And does not Wordsworth's greatness lie in his bearing witness, as we were about to lose it, to that age-old norm which in this century we have so largely destroyed, to our great loss and indeed to our great peril? But if we forget our cosmic ancestry are we not still

Rolled round in earth's diurnal course,
With rocks, and stones, and trees[?]

There have of course always been cities, of whose rise and fall
great civilizations have left the records. Epic poems have told
of the great and outstanding events and achievements of tribe
and nation. In the personae of Hamlet and Lear and Prospero,
Iago and Macbeth, Shakespeare has explored the bounds and
limits of human experience, as have the writings of Plato and
the sacred literature of India and Arabia. The religious and
epic literature of all civilizations has told of the exceptional, of
the farthest reaches of the human spirit. The grass roots were
always there and perhaps seemed to need no telling. Was
Wordsworth's decision to 'choose incidents and situations
from common life, and to relate or describe them throughout,
as far as possible, in a selection of language really used by men'
a response to the coming change which already threatened
that age-old norm? Had this choice of material been no more
than a political response to a changing society moving from
an aristocratic to a democratic structure its interest would have
been historical only. But that speech, that language Wordsworth bequeathed to us is in itself an inestimable treasure.
Modern demotic speech of our post-industrial world may be
'really used by men', but it is a rootless language reflecting not
so much humankind's immemorial experience over generations as our modern forgetfulness of these. It is an instant language fit for the communication of matters of fact rather than
our deeper and more permanent experiences. But this was not
the 'language really used' by the men and women of Wordsworth's Cumberland and Westmorland, to whose speech he
had listened from childhood. Being unlettered, theirs was a
spoken language inherited from an ancestral past, a regional
speech which, like every oral tradition, was attuned to the ear,

not a soundless language of 'the words on the page' as critics a few years ago used to say was the language of poetry. Indeed the language Wordsworth would have known—in common with all oral traditions—possessed many virtues already lost to written language, and still more to the modern media.

Free from the adulteration of external influences, words come, in any traditional society, from generation to generation laden with the experience and memories of family and tribe, wedding language to certain places, wedding people to the land itself, as indeed did the Border Ballads which constituted the oral tradition of Cumberland and Northumberland and adjacent Scotland. So the reality of memories and language was self-perpetuating, enhancing the collective and individual dignity of those who shared both language and culture. Such stable societies are now rare and in England no longer to be found. It is still possible to find—or to find those who still remember—in the Western Highlands of Scotland or in Ireland a living regional speech and culture. Fast vanishing as in every kitchen in the remotest croft or cabin the television set usurps the place of the bard and the story-teller who kept alive the language and the stories. English is now a world language, but with the acquisition of information gleaned from the entire planet speech has lost the resonance of ancestral memories of people inheriting words from their ancestors, and ancestral sanctities. In the Hebrides I have been told that Gaelic is 'the language of Eden'. That surely is not to be taken as a fact of philology, but in a symbolic sense as an affirmation of the primordiality of ancestral speech from time immemorial, with the continuity of memory before it became permeable by the new rootless tongue. Surely Wordsworth's 'language really spoken by men' would have been a variant of this immemorial 'language of Eden'. Such a language has been the expression of basic human experiences deeply undergone because no anodynes of our modern 'distraction from distraction by distraction' had anaesthetized hearts broken by guilt and sorrow, poverty, solitude, sickness, old age and death, those unchanging inescapable human griefs; and joy too comes simply, and love is for the near and known. Wordsworth's language common to men — at best a poetic diction capable of Biblical dignity and immemorial simplicity — he understood as a language common to men because it is the bearer of those universal deep experiences of life and death. He came near, surely, in seeking a language 'really spoken by men' not to a shared mediocrity but to the universal language of Eden. There is no anonymity in Milton's exalted speech, nor in Shelley's eloquence of the world of the soul, nor in Tennyson's smooth, nor in Browning's rough idiomatic speech. At best Wordsworth renders speech transparent in a common tongue commensurate with the dignity of unfallen Man. Perhaps one must go to America to find the like — Whitman, or even Robert Frost, heirs to no hampering poetic conventions; and dare I venture to use also the comparison with the simplicity and depth of language of the African American spirituals and the 'blues' — for the 'language of Eden', in this sense, is universal.

Few English poets have attained a language which to the same degree crosses barriers of class and education, a language deeply satisfying as such, even in the most diffuse passages of *The Prelude* and *The Excursion*. It carries us in its flow, the ordinary and the unusual inextricably mingled; it has the sustaining quality of ever present reality, carrying us on over hidden depths and rare illuminations, which would suffer by isolation from that whole texture, seamless, like life itself.

The grass roots of life had, when Wordsworth wrote, hitherto always survived the rise and fall of civilizations, in men and women whose lives were simple, but not mean or corrupted, whose skills of husbandman and shepherd satisfied

the needs not only of material survival, but also the instinc-
tive need to beautify life with music and dance, with flower
gardens such as Dorothy Wordsworth planted round Dove
Cottage, the arts of embroidery and wood-carving, the fur-
nishings of farm and cottage. And in many poems Wordsworth speaks of the courteous and thoughtful speech of the
old huntsman Simon Lee, or the lonely leech-gatherer, village
children, even vagrants on the road. Nor should we forget that
the King James Bible and the Book of Common Prayer raised,
from the sixteenth to the end of the nineteenth century, the
level of culture for all classes in England, for whom those
books formed perhaps their only reading, or who at least
habitually heard that simple and noble language weekly in
parish churches; a structure of minimal culture no longer available to the 'ordinary men' of the end of the twentieth century.
The demotic speech of our modern cities carries no memories of Eden nor current of sacred wisdom from the Christian
religion; rather it is the speech of a world that has ceased to
remember.

But none of this is surely in itself sufficient to account for the
profound transformative effect on the soul of the English
nation of which I am but one of the many who experienced its
power. At the time of his writing no doubt Wordsworth's
political enthusiasms found an echo which had more to do
with history than with poetry, and are in their nature transient
however transformative in the world of outer events. Milton
too had strong political affiliations, but who cares now, as
we read *Lycidas* or 'Il Penseroso' —or indeed *Paradise Lost*—
what these were? Or who cares whether Dante supported the
Guelphs or the Ghibellines? Whereas the moon setting over
Lucy's cottage, or an old shepherd in a fold of the hills who
went 'many and many a day' to the never to be finished sheep-

fold that years before he had planned with his son who had departed never to return 'And never lifted up a single stone'; or a schoolboy who 'blew mimic hootings to the silent owls' until they answered him; or that two boys rescued a lamb carried away in a flooded beck, are no less real to us than they were to Wordsworth. True, the pastoral Golden Age is an archetypal reality of the Imagination that never dies and Wordsworth's poetry is a retelling of that myth in terms of his time and place. But he was also the voice of a revolution of consciousness of a more profound kind, a reorientation of the national soul, hitherto sustained by the Christian religion within a framework of theological terms no longer adequate. Wordsworth's profound insight into nature was rather cosmological than theological. For better or worse Western Christianity has always been deeply suspicious of 'pantheism', preferring to keep creator and creation apart; never more so than in nineteenth century Deism, that 'natural religion' that acknowledged the creator of a universe that thereafter operated according to natural laws, which themselves were in due course to eliminate the divine life from the universe to give place to atheist materialism. But Wordsworth's living experience went beyond creed or reason in his 'Lines written a few miles above Tintern Abbey':

> a sense sublime
> Of something far more deeply interfused
> Whose dwelling is the light of setting suns,
> And the round ocean, and the living air,
> And the blue sky, and in the mind of man,
> A motion and a spirit, that impels
> All thinking things, all objects of all thought,
> And rolls through all things . . . .

The experience of the mystic—and surely Wordsworth's

was no less—went beyond those structures available to his time and place: for him 'nature' was alive, sometimes fearfully so, as for the boy who one evening loosed the chain of a little boat and pushed it out from the shore of Ullswater; and pleasure gave place to fear—

> When from behind that craggy Steep, till then
> The bound of the horizon, a huge Cliff
> Upreared its head. I struck and struck again
> And, growing still in stature, the huge Cliff
> For so it seemed, with purpose of its own,
> Rose up between me and the stars, and still,
> With measured motion, like a living thing
> Strode after me . . .
>   and after I had seen
> That spectacle, for many days, my brain
> Worked with a dim and undetermined sense
> Of unknown modes of being . . . .

Again we remember those lines from *The Prelude* in which Wordsworth describes the Simplon pass:

> Black drizzling crags that spake by the way-side
> As if a voice were in them, the sick sight
> And giddy prospect of the raging stream,
> The unfettered clouds and region of the heavens,
> Tumult and peace, the darkness and the light
> Were all like workings of one mind, the features
> Of the same face, blossoms upon one tree
> Characters of the great Apocalypse,
> The types and symbols of Eternity,
> Of first and last, and midst, and without end.

The gods of India would have been at home here!
    Janet Adam Smith and other mountaineers have rightly

compared this passage with Turner's great painting of the pass of St Gothard, as an expression for the vogue of the Sublime which had characterized painting for some time. While natural genius is not to be explained in terms of 'influences' one undercurrent of the time which played a part in Wordsworth's imaginative experience was surely the Greek revival, of which Thomas Taylor's translations of Plato, Plotinus and the greater part of the Neoplatonic literature into English for the first time is an important but neglected aspect. Doubtless some scholar might be able to establish evidence of the extent to which Wordsworth was indebted to the Platonic writers. Certainly the pre-existence of the soul so clearly affirmed in the 'Ode: Intimations of Immortality' witnessed in early childhood is taken directly from Plato:

> Our birth is but a sleep and a forgetting:
> The Soul that rises with us, our life's Star,
>   Hath had elsewhere its setting,
>   And cometh from afar:
>   Not in entire forgetfulness
> But trailing clouds of glory do we come
>   From God who is our home.

Plato in the Tenth Book of the *Republic* describes the descent of souls about to be generated on earth, who on their way cross 'the plain of oblivion' and 'the river of forgetfulness' of which all must drink. Some souls drink so deeply of this river as to forget entirely the heavenly world; others who drink less deeply reach this world 'not in entire forgetfulness'. And last of all, the souls are wafted to their birth 'like shooting stars'—every image in Wordsworth's memorable lines is taken from this famous passage. Throughout the writings of Plotinus also we find the image of the 'sleep' and forgetting of generated souls—forgetfulness of the eternal world, 'Of God who is our

home'. Such statements are purely Platonic: the pre-existence
of the soul has no part in Christian theology.

Blake too declared that to believe in the immortality of the
soul after death is not possible if not also before birth. Blake
actually knew Thomas Taylor, and his Arlington Court Tem-
pera is an illustration of Taylor's translation of Porphyry's *De
Antro Nympharum*, a treatise on the descent and return of souls
through the world of generation. Shelley, deeply imbued as he
was with the Platonic philosophy, held the same belief in the
soul's pre-existence:

> Is it that in some brighter sphere,
>> We part from those we meet with here?
> Or do we see the future pass
>> Across the present's clouded glass?

Wordsworth was not, like Shelley, a committed Platonist
and increasingly in his later years reverted to Christianity; but
in his famous *Ode* he echoes Plato's words which re-echo
through the Greek philosophers and poets, 'Who knows
whether to live be not to die, and to die to live?' Life is the
soul's 'death' or forgetfulness, yet 'haunted for ever by the
eternal mind'. In this world there remain

> those obstinate questionings
> Of sense and outward things,
> Fallings from us, vanishings;
> Blank misgivings of a Creature
> Moving about in worlds not realized,
> High instincts, before which our mortal Nature
> Did tremble like a guilty Thing surprized;
>> But for those first affections,
>> Those shadowy recollections
>>> Which, be they what they may,
> Are yet the fountain light of all our day.

Wordsworth describes the fall of the soul of which philosophers have written, not as a 'belief' but, according to the greatness of his genius, as a living experience

> Though inland far we be
> Our souls have sight of that immortal sea
> Which brought us hither.

Another, and recurring, Platonic—or rather Plotinian—theme is the one life that 'rolls through all things' in nature, from rock and star to the so-called living world. I believe that *Lines written in Early Spring* derives directly from Plotinus, *Ennead* 1:4, as translated by Thomas Taylor. Wordsworth's lines have the spontaneous simplicity of an immediate thought which had come to the poet from the 'grove' in which he 'heard a thousand blended notes', which inspired in him the conviction that even the very plants enjoyed pleasure:

> Through primrose-tufts, in that sweet bower,
> The periwinkle trailed its wreathes;
> And 'tis my faith that every flower
> Enjoys the air it breathes.

> The birds around me hopped and played:
> Their thoughts I cannot measure,
> But the least motion which they made
> It seemed a thrill of pleasure.

> The budding twigs spread out their fan,
> To catch the breezy air;
> And I must think, do all I can,
> That there was pleasure there.

Plotinus' theme is 'True Happiness'[1]—or 'felicity' as Taylor translates the word. Plotinus begins, as does Wordsworth,

---

1. [The author quotes from the MacKenna translation.]

with 'such beings as have the gift of music' — birds in other words — who 'finding themselves well off in other ways, they sing, too, as their nature is, and so their day is pleasant to them'. Plotinus goes on to say that felicity lies in attaining the fulfilment of 'some ultimate Term pursued by inborn tendency', and then 'nature in them comes to a halt, having fulfilled its vital course from a beginning to an end'. He then says that not only is happiness, in this sense, attributable to the animal world, but 'not withholding it even from the plants, living they too and having a life unfolding to a Term'. So whatever creature unfolds to the completion of its nature, says Plotinus, must be allowed to be happy: 'If pleasure be the Term, if here be the good of life, it is impossible to deny the good of life to any order of living things.'

Even Wordsworth's phrase 'do all I can' — which might seem to be an unnecessary phrase whose only purpose is to fill in a rhyme — may well reflect Plotinus' own reservations: 'It may be a distasteful notion' he writes 'this bringing-down of happiness so low as to the animal world — making it over, as then we must, even to the vilest of them and not withholding it even from the plants'. It seems that Plotinus also had 'done all he could' to avoid the conclusion that plants and the very lowest forms of life enjoy felicity. Had Blake too, who wrote that 'every particle of dust breathes forth its joy', read Plotinus' words?

Blake, who never lost 'the divine vision' as Wordsworth declares he did, to the day of his death, comments on the Preface to the 1815 edition of Wordsworth's poems, that 'Wordsworth must know that what he Writes Valuable is Not to be found in Nature'. It lies, according to Blake, in the Imagination. In this Blake was in accord with what one may call the orthodoxy of the Perennial Philosophy, as taught by the Platonists, and by Plotinus especially, and also by the Oriental philosophies, for whom mind is primary, and 'nature' a *māyā*, a world of appearances. According to Plotinus Nature images and reflects the soul; as Coleridge also understood.

No political liberation from external 'tyranny' can effect that transmutation of mortal life; Coleridge, philosopher that he was, understood that the alchemy can be transformative of nature with such feeling and fullness as did Wordsworth. Blake wrote that 'everything that lives is holy'. Wordsworth, in his greatest poetry, famously communicates that reality; and has so far communicated that vision as to make for many the Lake District a national shrine to this day, a holy land. Yeats has written that the imagination of a nation must be 'wedded' to the mountains and rivers and places of our native land, that a remote 'holy land' — as is the land of Israel for Christians — fails to achieve the consecration of our own 'holy places', a dimension without which the soul suffers perpetual exile. Surely no other English poet has in a comparable degree thus 'wedded' the Imagination to his native place, and in a lesser degree to the natural world wherever he found it.

Blake objected to lines from *The Excursion*

> How exquisitely the individual Mind
> . . . to the external World
> Is fitted: – & how exquisitely, too,
> Theme this but little heard of among Men
> The external World is fitted to the Mind.

One can see why Blake objected since for him 'Nature is Imagination Itself' and the 'external world' is a deadly illusion. But Wordsworth was surely expressing a truth, described in our own time by the French phenomenologist Gaston Bachelard in his remarkable books on the four Elements and the poetic Imagination, which continually discovers in nature its 'objective correlative'. No poet knew better than

Wordsworth how the mind is raised to elevated thoughts by mountain heights, calmed by the contemplation of still lakes, finds its correspondences in both the minute and in the vast, the violet and the star, as Imagination continually discovers its fitting symbols in the epiphanic flow of the world of nature daily opening before our eyes. The experience of this marriage between Imagination and the natural world is one to which Wordsworth continually returns; to a living experience of nature as *meaning*—not emblematic and arbitrary as in allegory, but a continual invitation to the beholder to communion with the great cosmic mystery and the microcosm of Man. His culture—the culture of his age, provided him with no adequate context for these profound experiences within Christian orthodoxy with its strange dread of 'pantheism'. His living experience did not accord with that creed, to which in his later years he attempted to conform his vision. Better had he had the courage of his own insights, and affirmed with Blake that the universe is 'all alive' and 'every particle of dust breathes forth its joy'. A belief more in accordance with our own 'New Age' than with the confident assurance of nineteenth-century materialism.

I believe those who assent to the description of Wordsworth's art as 'the egotistical sublime' have failed to understand that he was not recording his individual experiences because they were unique but because they were universal. He assumed the role of Everyman, because it is through the uniqueness of the individual self through whose mediation alone we perceive the world, singular to each yet common to all. He took on, in this sense, to explore his own particular ego, in the name of anonymity. The eye of universal consciousness receives only in the particular life what is our universal heritage. Byron surely was interested in his own story in a way that Wordsworth was not, otherwise than as a window on the world. And is it not when he is most personal—as in the Lucy poems—and in his solitary communings with Nature that Wordsworth is most universal, offering us images through which we can enter the world as he experienced it? I find no such egoism in the *Prelude*, or in his greatest poems, only in those afterthoughts of his later life in which, as David Jones puts it, the poet gives place to what the world tells us we 'ought to think' and should 'try to feel'. I have never been able to work my way through the Ecclesiastical Sonnets; but when Wordsworth trusted the experience he was unerring. Is not the sense of the sacred more perfectly conveyed in those lines describing his sister Dorothy *experiencing* the sparrow's nest than in all the sonnets?

> She looked at it and seemed to fear it;
> Dreading, tho' wishing, to be near it.

The sparrow's nest is a *temenos*, a sacred sanctuary of life, the thing itself, not an emblem or an allegory; Coleridge's 'translucence of the eternal in and through the temporal' which 'always partakes of the Reality which it renders intelligible'. Because he so fully experienced himself as 'sole heir of the whole world' Wordsworth was 'more than so, because men are in it who are everyone sole heirs' as well as he. Nature, as Wordsworth experienced her inexhaustible epiphany of wonders, is indeed everyman's heritage, whether born in the country or in the city; nor, even in the city, is Nature inaccessible to us; Wordsworth found it even on Westminster Bridge, and in a tree at the corner of Wood Street; and

> To me the meanest flower that glows can give
> Thoughts that do often lie too deep for tears.

𝒢 Index